Praise for

"*Stress and Success* is a must re   ̣1
lead others in high-stakes settings,   ̣eld
or in the corporate boardroom. Gro   ̣ience
and practice, this engaging book provide   ̣hensive
and highly readable overview of not just   to handle
stress, but how to leverage it for personal growth. Taken to
heart, the lessons conveyed in this book will improve
performance and life quality among those who face
significant stress in their day-to-day lives."
**Michael D. Matthews, Professor of Engineering
Psychology, United States Military Academy,
West Point.**

"Marines learn that success in battle is keeping a cool
head while throwing the enemy so off balance that
further fighting is futile. It's that cool head that prevails
in business and in life. Jonathan Brown went right to the
source – our most modern Marine Corps tactical thought
- interviewing our thinkers and reading their work. And
he re-traced our steps back to the most ancient
philosophers of war. Brown's ability to translate what
we've learned in war into how you can help yourself in
peace is masterful."
**Michael Duncan Wyly, Colonel, USMC (ret).
Executive Director, Bossov Ballet.**

"Stress is the scourge of modern living impacting
everyone from the high school student to the CEO, from
the housewife to the Marine. I have seen more careers at
best spoiled and at worst ruined by stress than I would
have believed possible. It is truly one of the biggest
blights on Western society. Yet, it is still difficult to
recognise the symptoms and even harder to admit to it

and talk about it. This book, written by a man who has experienced and dealt with extreme stress, addresses these issues in a pragmatic and readable way. This should be a mandatory read for every busy person."
John Molter, Vice President, Global Customer Business Development, Procter & Gamble (Ret.)

"The 20th century's most influential strategist, the late Air Force Col John Boyd, counselled that because we could not eliminate confusion, a better idea was to make our opponents more confused than we were. Jonathan Brown, drawing on Boyd and many others, takes this a step further: Because we can't eliminate stress, our best tactic is to learn how to use it better than our competitors. Brown offers a comprehensive program for achieving this goal, pages of strategies and techniques that you can start using today and continue for a lifetime."
Chet Richards, Author of *Certain to Win* and long term collaborator with John Boyd.

"A must read for anyone with a busy and stressful life!"
Dr Paul A Brogan Reader in Vasculitis and Consultant Paediatric Rheumatologist, ICH and GOSH NHS Foundation Trust.

"Jonathan Brown is one of the finest coaches in Europe. This book provides a wonderful introduction to one of the many areas in which he provides expertise and enlightenment. It offers much useful advice as well as practical tools to deal with a broad variety of stress related issues."
Gary Leboff, Sports Psychologist, Author of Dare-Take on Your Life and Win.

"Jonathan Brown has written an impressive volume on how to handle stress, building on his personal experience and years of helping clients with stress problems. The book relies heavily on data from military operations, as well as from the scientific literature on the psychological factors that decide whether you cope with stress and thrive, or lose and succumb to misery."
Dr Holger Ursin, Professor emeritus, Uni health, University of Bergen, Norway.

"Wisdom can come from those who have 'been there' or have 'read widely'. Jonathan is one of those rare people who has achieved high performance in both, and has therefore achieved mastery. Written with compassion, breadth, depth and humanity, but with a cutting practical edge; there is something in Stress and Success for any leader who has been stressed, i.e. all of us! I highly recommend this book."
Nigel Cushion, Chairman, nelsonspirit.

"John Boyd died more than fifteen years ago. Since then a second generation of brilliant men has come along to advance, expand, and deepen Boyd's ideas. Jonathan Brown now moves into the forefront of those men with this new book. As startling as it is revelatory, this is a book I want to read again and again. It insures that Boyd's ideas will live on."
Robert Coram, Author of Boyd: The Fighter Pilot Who Changed The Art of War.

"The Fast Moving Consumer Goods market is getting faster and faster. The rapid development and deployment of new technologies supporting suppliers and retailers means that change is inevitable. For many people, constant change equals increased stress - at work and play. Jonathan's book aims to turn such stress into

an advantage. It's a form of mental alchemy which has got to be essential reading!"
Steve J. Smith - Director of Sales, AG Barr plc.

"You may think the topic doesn't apply to you but you're wrong. This book applies to everyone. Jonathan helps you to recognise the signs of stress which is a massive first step. Making the changes necessary to maintain success in tougher situations is an even bigger one. Thankfully, that is where I found Jonathan's advice most helpful. An excellent book."
Neil Marwood, Finance Director, Plasmor plc.

"Balancing multiple professional priorities and pressures alongside important personal commitments in today's complex workplace environment can make for a very challenging lifestyle. *Stress and Success* pulls out practical and real guidance on finding and maintaining a healthy life balance. Listening and acting on it can positively impact your life and improve your leadership."
Matthew Crummack, President of the lastminute.com Group.

"Of the many books I have read on extreme stress and its effects, Jonathan's approach in providing clear and sometimes amusing examples makes this a Number One read. A simple approach to Sleep, Activity and Nutrition is easily over looked as the keys to success in life. He brings it all home in a focused and delightful way-you can simply improve your life and that of your family once you embrace his suggestions."
Colonel Jill W. Chambers, US Army. (R) P.T.S.D. Pioneer and Founder of This Able Vet.

"This book is a terrific mix of practical wisdom and illuminating stories. The answer to workplace stress turns out not to be deep breathing or meditation, but a focus on mastery through engagement, focus, and capacity building. Top performers need to experience forward momentum in meaningful work, so managers should manage for progress. Stretch and recover, fill your life with appreciation - and refuse that extra muffin! **Paul Z. Jackson, Author of The Inspirational Trainer and The Solutions Focus**.

Within this book Jonathan utilises the wisdom of highly successful people, research into high performance, personal experience and good common sense to create a resource that is entertainingly educational and highly practical. Refreshingly, he does not offer a 'formula', more a range of areas it might be worth exploring. Like all good 'guides' in life he may offer many 'pointers' yet leaves the decisions to you. He wants you to avoid all the pitfalls he experienced yet he knows that these pitfalls may offer invaluable learning and therefore provides approaches to enable you to experience them and still grow. **David Whitaker O.B.E., Olympic Gold Medal winning coach and business coaching pioneer.**

"I have had the good fortune to collaborate with Jonathan Brown, and his common-sense approach to stress leadership is both highly effective and immediately useful. You can take the lessons from this book and employ them right away. I can't recommend Stress and Success any more highly!" **Lt. Colonel Mike Grice, US Marine Corp, (Ret.).**

Stress and Success

Fast Fixes for Turbulent Times

To Julie,

One of my leadership inspirations.

Jonathan

Copyright © 2013 by Jonathan Brown

All rights reserved. No part of this publication may be reproduced, stored in a retrieval system or transmitted, in any form or by any means, electronic, mechanical, photocopying, or otherwise, without prior permission of the Copyright owner.

The right of Jonathan Brown to be identified as the author of this work has been asserted by him in accordance with the Copyright, Designs and Patents Act, 1988.

Published by
EE (Publishing) Ltd,
The White House,
Marsworth,
Aylesbury Vale,
HP23 4LT.

ISBN: 978-1-849-14334-9

Cover design by Steven Costello

Dedication–Our Armed Forces and their Families

I will be donating profits from this book to UK and US armed forces personnel for two reasons. My first reason is simply to express my gratitude for their service. Sincerely, thank you.

My second reason is more personal–I know that families can pay a high price when their men (and women) go to war. I would like very much to help reduce that price. My grandfather, Flight Sergeant George "*Jimmy*" Brown, died in World War II. He left an adoring, pregnant 19-year-old wife who never fully recovered from losing him. This loss exacerbated the secondary effects of my great-grandfather's service in World War I. My grandmother told me that he could be calm and seemingly normal and then become deeply erratic and often violent. His behaviour was so intense that it still scared her decades after his passing.

Her stories about my great-grandfather contain many of the symptoms of what we now call Post Traumatic Stress. People write how fortunate we were not to have a PTSD problem in the UK after the two World Wars. My own family's experience makes me think that we were simply much more skilled at keeping things quiet and offering genuine community care.

I know from personal experience that unresolved psychological trauma from fighting in wars can affect families for generations. We didn't have this insight 95 years ago and people didn't get the help they needed. Now we do know and we have no excuse. The people who perform society's toughest tasks shouldn't be made to pay for the rest of their lives because we cannot or will not prepare them well enough for what they face in our name. I want this book to help some of those invisible heroes and their families who live among us.

Before this story, another...

The Man Who Could Fly

A man is inspired by flight and works tirelessly to find a way to fly unassisted. He finally figures out how to do it and proudly sends off his theories for publication in the world's top scientific journals.

He is amazed to find that other scientists don't believe him. In fact, they ridicule his ideas. Saddened but not entirely surprised, he tells the public. Yet they too laugh at him.

So he decides to show them. He invites the scientists, the public and the press to come and see him demonstrate his theories and climbs the tallest skyscraper in the city. With neither fanfare nor hesitation, he launches himself off the roof.

As he drops past the 50th storey he is heard to shout:

"So far, so good!"

Stress and Success:
Fast Fixes For Turbulent Times

1.
Introduction

The purpose of this book is simple. I want to help you to improve your ability to anticipate and recover from turbulent situations in a way that strengthens you for tomorrow's challenges. I have developed a different approach to stress incorporating science, business, and military theory and practice. It can help you to quickly recover from short-term challenges, improve your ability to handle future stressors, and then choose the types of stress that you are best suited to handle in the future. I call this s*tress leadership*[1] to highlight the bizarre situation that stress is the only place where executives want management and not leadership.

The problems we face with stress today can't be solved at the level at which most of us are working. Stress is really a symptom of a deeper challenge—how can we live successfully in a complex, turbulent world that is changing faster than our historic or natural rate of evolution? Some stress management techniques can help release resources but they can't answer this deeper question. The great news is that with mostly subtle adjustments you can quickly get ahead, and can start to turn the stress and the situation to your advantage. This different view of stress and how you can use it to be successful takes some time to develop. I promise that it is worth the effort.

There are three books in this series. This one is primarily tactical, helping you have a more profitable relationship with stress and success in the next 90 days. The strategic drivers to help you generate long-term sustained and sustainable success are all present but the focus is on immediate application, faster adaptation and reducing the short term price you pay to achieve your goals. As this short term work will give you the resources and outlook to be able to tackle bigger stressors, it's the place to start if you are planning significant performance improvement.

Book two looks further ahead and helps you to discern longer term trends and opportunities. It contains ideas for accelerating learning and performance by matching your aims with your broader environment. Book three looks at how you can generate long term success with others by actively shaping the environment to suit you and those around you.

I weave a number of ideas and theories together, so some theoretical explanation is essential, but I have worked to keep visible theory as light as possible. I have cut a lot of additional content and exercises to keep the book size manageable. I have placed much of this on the website for the series: www.stressandsuccess.com.

Why Is a Stress and Success Focus Worth Your Time?

Professor Hans Selye, who was probably the most important pioneer of stress research, defined stress as *"the rate of all the wear and tear caused by life."*[2] Selye showed that most of it is avoidable, even though the rate seems to be intensifying. This is reassuring as a high enough rate can push us into a downward spiral.

The potentially severe consequences of this downward spiral offer excellent reasons for adopting a more dynamic approach to stress. Prolonged exposure to negative stress has been linked with accelerated aging, decreased bone density (and increased osteoporosis), reduced muscle mass, reduced skin growth and regeneration, impaired immune function, increased blood sugar, and increased adipose tissue (fat accumulation around waist and hips).

Stress Makes You Ill

These short-term maladaptations can lead to a smorgasbord of all the major modern illnesses—obesity, diabetes, infertility, hypertension, heart disease, cancer, and Alzheimer's. The medical consequences alone suggest that small investments in further improving what is likely to be an already high-stress tolerance will pay personal long-term dividends. Yet, as compelling as these reasons may be, I don't think that is why you should make stress leadership a priority. So why do I think learning to lead your response to stress is worth your time?

Increased challenge and stress are here to stay. We are facing continued cost pressures for at least the next five years. The recession has accelerated the shift in relative economic strength to Asia. This means that most of us will be facing genuinely global competition for the first time. Being able to handle higher levels of stress than your competition and turning a turbulent situation to your advantage will be immensely helpful abilities in shrinking markets awash with overcapacity. To lead in these more turbulent situations, you need to be able to think clearly when everything and maybe everyone around you is going crazy. This brings me to the most important reason why you should focus on this area.

Stress Causes Viral Stupidity

Perhaps the most important reason to get serious about stress is to counteract the way it reduces the quality of your thinking. Stress impairs your memory, your ability to think, to learn, and to solve problems. Most of us are paid for our thinking, so this cognitive impairment *(a.k.a. viral stupidity)* is career limiting. If you lead or manage others, it is worth noting that *viral stupidity* is contagious, i.e. one person can infect others and turn a whole team temporarily daft. The principles in this book will help you minimise that possibility.

The conventional view of stress is unhelpful for today's realities and is just as likely to make your long-term problems worse as it is to make them better. In this book, I'd like to explain why this is so and suggest a different approach that allows you to behave more skilfully and flexibly in turbulent times that prepares you for future challenges.

Working in Hostile Environments

I am not referring to war time settings here but the world we have created for ourselves. We used to be able to take a supportive (or benign) environment for granted. This is no longer the case. We are now able to do things routinely for which neither we nor our ancestors have any history. For example, we have no real experience of being on all the time, flying across time zones, working under pressure 18 hours a day in a room with artificial light and air, eating processed food, being exposed daily to persistent and ubiquitous chemicals and then flying through the night to get home for the weekend to be with our families.

I am not suggesting that we should return to some idyllic, imaginary past. I am suggesting that to get the amazing benefits of the lives many of us can lead today, we need to take more personal responsibility for the consequences of our choices. We need to check just how safe or desirable it really is for us to do what we can do. For example, to stay healthy after choosing the international executive life briefly described above, we need to appreciate the cost of constant adaptation and be much more deliberate about our recovery. We need to take control of the externalities of our lifestyles. Otherwise we can find ourselves in immensely hostile situations of our own making.

We are All Tow–in Surfers

An analogy I use on my programs to demonstrate the danger of getting into hostile environments is the amazing sport of tow-in surfing. This is the sport where a surfer is towed on the back of a jet-ski into the path of an enormous wave–a wave they would be unable to paddle out to themselves without the use of technology.

As surfers develop their craft, their paddling skills develop in line with their surfing skill. The paddling skills give you increased awareness of the sea, how the waves are breaking and where the sea is pushing, and increases your ability to predict how a wave will develop and which wave to choose–essential if you want to stay safe in the water.

However, as the jet-ski has reduced the need for skillful paddling, you can no longer assume that a surfer has the skill to handle the wave. If you are unconcerned or unaware of the risks, have sufficient motivations (or if you are daft enough), you can get yourself into potentially lethal situations surprisingly easily. This is the same with our lives today. Consequently, we need to strengthen our choice making to match the potential opportunities and threats in our environment. Just because we can do something, doesn't mean we should.

Stress Management Won't Help For Long

A popular view is that is that stress is experienced when:

Perceived challenge > perceived resources.

This can help us and we will use this definition at times throughout the book. However, there are a few embedded assumptions in the challenge-resource definition that are worth making explicit. The core one is that flaws in your thinking (perceptual distortions) are the main cause of stress, for example, anxiety, fear, lack of self-belief. This means that you have the resources to deal with the situation you just don't think you do. Therefore, change your thinking, end the stress. This seems so simple we may wonder what all the fuss is about....

Techniques such as reframing or some form of cognitive behavioural therapy (where you learn to see things differently–"it's not a *problem, it's a challenge*"), and mind-clearing techniques, such as breathing and relaxation can help with this one type of stress (which I will explain soon). And we will be using some traditional techniques to help prevent viral stupidity.

What they can't do is secure long-term success. This is because they seek to address what is assumed to be a temporary problem in isolation. That is, your stressor will end soon and has no connection to anything else you are doing. Thinking about the problems you deal with today versus the ones you dealt with one, two, or five years ago, how true is this? Are your challenges bigger or smaller? Do you actually believe the stress is going to end any time soon? Will your life be easier in a year's time? How about in a decade?

So stress management won't solve the bigger issue but we can and will use it to have a better day. And helping you to deal more effectively with single stressors and tough days will free up the resources for you to be able to recover and to invest in the kinds of skills you will need to remain successful throughout the next economic cycle. So there's nothing wrong with stress management as long as we use it to help with single events.

Get Ahead of the Curve

So the problem isn't really traditional stress management, it's just that *we are only managing when we need to be leading.* In recognising that we are facing VUCA environments, to use a military term– environments that are volatile, uncertain, complex, and ambiguous–we need to adapt in a way that helps us today *and* in a way that improves our ability to adapt in the future.[3]

We need to manage the moment and use the free resources to lead our future building activities. We can then build a coherent strategy for winning that increases our competence and capacity and strengthens alliances. If I can help you to see what may be heading your way you will have the chance to prepare or even avoid the problem completely. You can choose to avoid some waves or even find a different beach. And you could also use any turbulence to exploit the fleeting opportunities that emerge in these situations.

Resources v Resourcefulness

The other issue with using only this definition is that it makes no reference to the level of resourcefulness you apply to the resources you have. *"I am stronger than this,"* is a confident statement that relates mostly to the resources you have. Imagine saying this as you *wrestle* the stressor to the ground.

"I'm faster and more adaptable than this," relates to how you apply your resources, i.e. your resourcefulness. And if you are faster and more adaptable you may be able to avoid the wrestling completely. Imagine saying this as you *dance* with the stressor instead of fighting with it. How much less expensive would that be? This focus on resourcefulness is at the core of all productivity improvement– doing things differently to do more with what you have. This book is all about improving your speed and adaptability. If you can improve speed and adaptability enough, you will be able to move at a higher tempo than the situation. This will give you the power to

choose how you interact so that you can choose to dance instead of fight.

Test, Test and Test Again

My insights will help only if they improve your own understanding and actions. As Piaget defined it, I need to help you to develop your capacity *to figure out what to do when you don't know what to do.* To do this, you need to test things for yourself.

One of the defining characteristics of turbulent or dynamic environments is that they can't be understood through traditional analysis and observation. They move so fast that as soon as you leave the events in the environment to take time to "understand" them, they will have moved on and won't be the same when you return. These environments have to be experienced as you maintain and improve your awareness of what is happening in the moment. This ensures your solutions remain relevant. Therefore, you need to actively interact with your environment through rapid testing and shorter feedback cycles (the time it takes to find out if your ideas work). It is only through these tests that you can gather the data you need to understand what is happening. So, as a general rule, if you are in doubt about anything in this book (and even if you are certain), test quickly and cheaply and then reapply the learning.

Focus on the Next 90 Days

To get the most out of the book, I suggest you focus not on changing or transforming your life but on making the next 90 days or so better than the last 90 days. There are simple ideas you can apply immediately. The results you get will give you reassurance you are on the right track and persuade you to make bigger, longer term investments. It doesn't have to be 90 days but it does need to be at least 45 days. This gives you a full month with additional time to reapply the learning from your tests in the next monthly cycle of events. To make this real, choose a time period that works for you and start the clock on your focus on improving your ability to handle turbulent situations now.

Apply Key Ideas Consistently

To generate momentum, I help my clients to quickly identify some core tactics or strategies that they can apply consistently. Warren Buffet, the world's most successful investor (and by all accounts one of the happiest men on the planet) said this about a lesson he gained from his mentor, Ben Graham:

"Ben Graham taught me 45 years ago that in investing it is not necessary to do extraordinary things to get extraordinary results. In later life, I have been surprised to find that this statement holds true in business management as well. What a manager must do is handle the basics well and not get diverted." [4]

This applies to every situation I have succeeded in. By consistently applying sound principles and allowing only affordable or acceptable losses, you can quickly transform your performance. In the next 90 days, find ways to handle the right basics well and reduce diversions.

When you get stressed, you resort to your most ingrained habits. Therefore, how you act in stressful situations must be consistent with your most ingrained day-to-day habits. If different, you won't be able to act quickly enough in turbulent situations as your habits won't be strong enough to stand the pressure. This means that "*stress management*" can't be something you do every so often. It has to be integrated into your daily work.

It's also possible to use popular management tools and techniques that you use in your business. I have found that many can be adapted to personal use. For example, you can apply cash flow management principles to *"energy flow management."* This helps you and your team immediately but also educates them in a vital business skill. This increases your return on your investment in stress leadership.

Why Can You Trust What I Say?

The ideas in this book have come from a number of places. In order of importance, they are:

1. **My burn out and recovery.** I burnt out during the early stages of the Great Financial Crash (GFC) as my property business and consultancy both crashed. I suffered massive problems both personally (including an 18-month depression and 30kg weight gain) and financially (losing about $1m). I mention some of these experiences in the book when relevant, but I don't dwell on them. However, my experiences during this time are relevant to our dialogue. They showed me that the most popular ideas on performance and stress don't work when you really need them. This was a painful and expensive lesson.

To recover I had to figure out what did work. I have and I am now in better shape (in every way) than I have been in my adult life. I know from personal experience just how you can reverse stress- or age-related damage. You can be confident that my experience and learning can help you with the challenges that you face. And take reassurance that even though some situations can't be fixed, you can nearly always recover from them as I have.

2. **Research into in-extremis performers.** I wonder if you have ever heard a manager say something like this:

"When my people get stressed, I say "Don't worry. Our work's not that important—at least no one died."

However well-intentioned these statements, if you are like me, you probably feel uncomfortable with that approach. In saying that, we unintentionally reduce the perceived importance of someone's work which can reduce motivation. If it isn't important, why do we make the sacrifices we do?

Have you ever wondered what people whose work can lead to someone dying say and do—when work is literally life and death? I did and began studying *"in-extremis"* or high–stakes performers—specifically the military, emergency services, surgeons, and airline pilots. They deal with situations that are much more consequential than financial crises. What do they do?

Many suffer more than my corporate clients but others are applying some terrific tools that are literally battle-tested. I have studied how those people do and don't deal with stress and pressure, and have transferred the relevant lessons back to a corporate environment. Once you deal with the differences between normal situations and life and death situations, you have a set of incredibly useful ideas and insights that will stand the intense scrutiny turbulence can generate.

This research into high stakes situations brought me to the philosophical underpinnings of maneuver warfare—the dynamic, disruptive and agile approach to combat practiced by the US Marine Corps and just about any Special Force around the world today. This is an ancient body of study which is focused on how to dynamically address potential conflict in the most challenging environments in the world. I have taken some of these strategies and applied them in working environments. They transfer brilliantly.

I have paid particular attention to a US philosopher best known for his military work, John Boyd. What is less well known is that Boyd's best and most useful ideas came after his retirement from the military. During this time, he focused on how to win in peaceful environments. I'll be drawing on those ideas most of all.

3.   **My corporate work.** Today I am fortunate to work with some of the smartest and most stressed people on the planet. Most of my work is helping high achievers get even better at handling difficult situations for less cost to themselves and their families. This involves helping leaders to create more supportive environments for their people to deliver their best work with less negative stress. For a few clients, I help engineer extremely fast performance turnarounds/recoveries and do for them in 3 months what took me 18 months to do on my own.

My reason for telling you where my ideas have come from is that I want to earn just enough of your trust up front so that you are willing to test some of these ideas out for yourself. I know the ideas have a firm, albeit unconventional foundation. I know they work as I use them myself and with clients every day. You don't have this experience yet so the testing is crucial for you to feel confident you are on the right track.

There is No Magic Pill

I prefer most of my client income to be performance related–the better you do, the better I do. This motivates me to figure out the fastest solutions so you can get on and I can leave. However, there is no magic pill for turbulent situations. I will give you the practical tools and materials to build a bridge between where you are now and where you want to be. *You need to build the bridge.* At times, overcoming old habits and constraints will be hard work. But the impact of applying those tools and ideas consistently builds exponentially over the next 3 months.

In all my work, I follow what two of my favourite business authors[5] have described as *Pfeffer's Law* and *Sutton's Law.*

Pfeffer's Law

Instead of being interested in what is new, we ought to be interested in what's true.

Sutton's Law

If you think that you have a new idea, you are wrong. Someone probably already had it. This idea isn't original either; I stole it from someone else.

This is a posh way of telling you that some of my advice may sound like things your grandmother would say. This is because the advice is still true and that she was right! I make no claims for originality. I do make claims for effectiveness.

There will be some tools or techniques that you are using in one part of your life that would work equally well in others. You just need to apply them more consistently. Also, if you are like my clients, you will have stopped applying a lot of the ideas in this book when your challenge and stress started to build. I hope to help you renew what you do in challenging situations so that you can be the wiser version of yourself more often in the next 90 days. I encourage you to review what used to work as it may still be of service. That way, you don't have to learn too many new ideas, just new ways of using old ones more consistently. This tends to be a much faster way to improve performance.

Doctor Rules

I am not qualified to give medical advice and nothing in this book should be construed as such. If you are experiencing high levels of stress or are unsure how serious your stress is, speak with your doctor. Health professionals helped me. They may do the same for you.

Striving for Success Without the Suffering

My experiences, and I hope my example, demonstrate that with relatively small yet profound changes consistently applied, you can find ways to deliver excellence without having to sacrifice yourself or those around you. It may be too much to say that we can have it all, but we can certainly have *success without the suffering.*

The Way Forward

The plan for the rest of the book (and the next 90 days) is to focus on what I call the first two ABCs of stress and success. These are:

(0-1 day): Master the moment and improve your immediate response to stress. Specifically:

1. **Anticipate and Accelerate** more effectively as you meet a challenge,
2. Improve your **Braking** to slow your stress response where helpful,
3. Reduce the **Cost** of your actions and prepare yourself for the next challenge.

The second set of ABCs (which overlap the first) are designed to help you from 0–90 days:

1. **Accumulate and attract resources** to improve your capacity and capability for handling turbulence. This will help you to choose how you respond to challenges and potential stressors.
2. **Brain Function**–Support and structure your thinking so that you can maintain perspective, deepen your environmental awareness, think clearly, and avoid "progress traps."[6]
3. **Care and Support**–Ensure you get (and give) the help and support needed for you and those you care about to tackle the challenges ahead.

Where would you like to go next?

Some of my clients simply want to start changing things, others want more understanding. Whatever your desire, I encourage you to read and apply chapters 2-4 first. This gives you an outline of the different approach I have developed, deepens your understanding of the stress and success you currently experience and gives you some ideas for getting more success and less stress immediately. After that you can go where you like. If the chapter is long, I break it into sections.

The ABCs do overlap but the key ideas for mastering the moment with better acceleration and braking are mostly contained in chapters 4, 5 and 7.

I add some theory that helps explain why the first ABC works and how you can take the ideas further with the second ABCs. Chapter 6 gives you more on the brain and how your emotions help and hinder your performance. Chapter 7 shows you how to develop more coherence and influence over your entire physiology. This is a core skill for mastering the moment but I have placed it there as I have found people to be more receptive when they get more of the science first. It's also a crucial long term skill.

Chapters 8-12 focus on the second ABC. Chapter 8 will help you to accumulate and attract the resources you need to be more effective. Chapters 9 and 10 give you a deeper understanding of military theory and how you can improve brain function in challenging situations. This will help you to minimise the chances of suffering viral stupidity.

Chapter 11 gives you ways to be your own source of positive emotions. This can dramatically increase long term resilience.

You can read them and apply the learning in whichever order most suits you.

2.
Winning and Losing:
What Stress Could Mean

In this chapter, I will briefly explain why stress occurs. I will then share the meaning, mind-set and approach to stress that determines if the effect of that stress is positive or negative. I will give some suggestions for maximising positive stress and minimising unnecessary or unhelpful distress.

Why does Stress Occur?

This is the answer I work with:

Stress occurs when there is a mismatch between the immediate demands of our environment and our capacity and desire to adapt and recover.

A favourable mismatch (where our desire and capacity are greater than the demands) leads to positive stress (or **eustress** as Hans Selye described it). We have the resources and the resourcefulness to meet the immediate demands of our environment. We can then choose to invest the surplus capacity or desire to achieve better results today or to invest in things that will help us recover faster and win tomorrow. We will have a greater sense of freedom to engage in and win the games we deem important. Our tempo and adaptive energy is greater than the demands of the situation. We gain more choice and we win. A consistent surplus and an intelligent strategy can sometimes create the opportunity to actually shape our environment to suit our purpose.

If the balance is against us, and we have insufficient capacity or willingness to engage as the situation demands, **distress** builds and we fall behind. The environment then starts to shape us, and our freedom to act is curtailed (sometimes fatally). The story can then go one of two ways. A high level of distress can lead to permanent damage, such as a career-ending physical injury for an athlete. If we are fortunate, and the distress is only just too much, it can lead to development (if we have the time to recover before the next challenge).

We may have suffered and lost today, but we can still win tomorrow as the lessons can build capacity and even desire. Our distress would be like a fitness regime which is temporarily distressing and exhausting but will make us stronger if we have exercised at the appropriate level. The key question is: will we get another chance to reapply this learning?

Winning Equals Making Progress

Hans Selye said a stressor is essentially neutral. Our experience of eustress or distress is a result of whether we believe we are winning or losing. This links extremely well to the *Progress Principle*, developed recently by Harvard Business School Professor Teresa Amabile and psychologist Steven Kramer.[7]

Amabile and Kramer discovered that top performers need to experience *"forward momentum in meaningful work,"* and they suggest managers should manage for progress. And the philosopher John Boyd suggested that our motivation for doing anything was to:

"Survive on our own terms, or improve our capacity for independent action."[8]

All three bodies of research demonstrate the importance of how we explain to ourselves what we are doing, why you are doing it, and our interpretation of the results we get. There is considerable leeway for each of us to decide if something is meaningful or not. Consequently, your explanations and interpretations of events are things to consider as you develop your stress leadership.

Winning and losing, survival on your own terms, or eustress and distress are answers to the same question. Sadly, most companies, in their efforts to help stressed employees, focus only on reducing distress–helping their people to avoid losing. It's actually crucial to get everyone in the firm to review how they win or experience eustress because it's this that generates the profit. Leaders should look at their approach to winning, their relevant skill levels, and how they influence their own desire to do the job. This works at an organizational level as much as it does for making progress in your own life. If you can develop more successful strategies that are in harmony with your environment, you can avoid a great deal of negative stress in the short term and dramatically increase the possibility of much more eustress in the long term.

In addition to the strategies you are using to interact with your environment, it is important to look at the quality of the relationships you have with others. Collaborative working is usually crucial in challenging and complex situations because the effort required to win is usually too much for one person. Collaborative working is particularly difficult in stressful situations as most of us tend to tighten up and attempt to do more ourselves rather than look around and see who else can help. To be able to improve collaboration in stressful situations, we must have already made it our default way of behaving because only the most ingrained habits can stand intense stress. (I'll focus on this in Chapter 4.)

What Makes Getting What You Want so Difficult?

Recall the last time you set a challenging goal. Now read the next paragraph and see if it resonates.

> "...<u>Winning</u> becomes extremely difficult because of the countless factors that impinge on it. These factors have collectively been called friction...Friction is the force that resists all action and saps energy. It makes the simple difficult and the difficult seemingly impossible...Only through experience can we come to appreciate the force of will [desire] necessary to overcome friction and to develop a realistic appreciation for what is possible <u>to win</u> and what is not."[9]

Does that make sense? In the situation you recalled, was the biggest problem knowing what to do or actually doing it? Nearly all my clients say it was doing the work–turning the ideas into reality that was the hardest thing. Knowing what to do wasn't anywhere near as hard.

Now, the above passage is actually adapted from the US Marine Corps handbook on how to win in combat, *Warfighting.* To be true to the source, you need to change the underlined words for "*war*" and "*in war.*" I have found the logic holds in business. To win, you must address the friction or stress in the marketplace. This means not only tackling it but either finding a way to turn it to your advantage, or to make it harder for your competition to succeed than it is for you.

Diversions and Stress Are Unavoidable

There is too much complexity and too many constraints for us to ever generate a perfect match with our environment. Thinking about the Warren Buffet quote in the last chapter–"*handle the basics well and [don't] get diverted*"—we can now see that diversions and negative stress will be inevitable. There will always a mismatch of some kind so there will always be stress. This means that how you interact with your environment and what is happening around you is pivotal to your ability to succeed in the long term.

Karl Popper once argued in an essay entitled, "*All life is problem solving*," that "*error correction was the most important method in technology and learning in general.*"[10] Often the errors you need to correct are the ones you have created through your solutions to earlier problems. Popper stressed that having to correct your own errors was inevitable and essential as life too dynamic, complex and ambiguous for you to have the time and resources to produce a perfect answer. All solutions lead to externalities. Seeing these externalities as tomorrow's work can reduce the stress you experience when you realize you have created another fine mess! *Recovery is more important than perfection.*[11] Instead of trying to be perfect work hard to make progress and to quickly correct errors you made in good faith. These errors can actually help you to move forward.

Chris Argyris and Donald Schon also focused on error correction as a key way to reduce the mismatch between our expectation and our experiences.[12] Anything that surprises (both positively and negatively) is worth investigating as the surprise highlights a gap in our understanding. Sadly, this helpful investigation into surprises is something that we stop doing when stressed as it requires resources we feel we do not have to spare.

Can We See Stress as Feedback?

Change causes friction—which leads to stress (as the Marines said). What if you saw the cause of this friction as the real challenge? If stress is caused by a mismatch between you and your environment, you could see the stress as feedback on how well you are interacting with it. It's an assessment of the effectiveness of your strategy for winning. A good strategy will help you win by addressing the environmental demands, challenges, and constraints. This means you can stop seeing stress as an undesirable but inevitable part of corporate life–like dealing with the trash in the office. Instead, the friction is the reason you have a job. If there was no mismatch, there'd be no need for your work. It's important then to review your strategy or approach to winning both as an individual and for your company to resolve the causes of any significant mismatches.

Positive and Negative Feedback

Most people have forgotten what positive and negative feedback were meant to be. Today, positive feedback is typically regarded as something that's nice to hear and negative feedback is something that is bad to hear. People often apologise when giving negative feedback.

If we are genuinely committed to embracing reality both types of feedback should be equally welcome, as long as we have time to reapply it. This is easier to accept when we remember where the phrases actually came from and what they used to mean.

Simply, the concepts of positive and negative feedback came from electrical circuitry via cybernetics. Positive feedback, in an electrical circuit, is something that reinforces the movement of energy around the circuit. This helps it to flow even faster and more smoothly. We could call it "*reinforcing feedback.*" Negative feedback is energy that travels against the direction of the energy in the circuit. This impedes future energy flows. You could call this "*impeding feedback.*"

Either one could help you to reduce the mismatch between you and your environment. If you give or get positive feedback, the goal is to get more of what you liked and increase harmony in the system. This reinforces the energy moving around the "circuits" you want to encourage. If you give or get negative feedback, you are simply looking to help stop behaviours or actions that cause mismatches, to reduce the disharmony. The aim in dynamic situations is to simply get the feedback you need to spot and then correct errors or mismatches before they do any serious damage. So negative or positive feedback is fine. The real danger is running out of the time you need to correct the errors.

Recognise and Tackle Different Levels of Distress

As we can never have perfect harmony and a perfect strategy, negative stress is inevitable. So let's take a closer look at that now. Rob Archer, a psychologist based in London, argues that companies addressing negative employee stress usually try to reduce it at three levels–distraction, disengagement, and distress.[13] Given the recovery work I do, I have introduced a fourth "D" beyond distress–damage. I reproduce all four levels in Figure 1 with Rob's agreement.

Figure 1. The Four "Ds" of Stress

| Damaged | Distressed | Disengaged | Distracted |

These four levels represent an ascending spectrum of trouble from right to left. You begin your journey through these levels by being merely distracted. You still manage to deliver your results despite slightly impaired thinking, 20 to 30 fluid priorities, and a personal life that is as busy as your professional life. As the level of distraction increases though, you find yourself disengaging in an attempt to minimize the discomfort of an increasingly overwhelming situation.

This disengagement causes further separation and isolation between you and your environment. You unconsciously begin to reduce efforts to influence what is happening for two reasons.

1. You become concerned or fearful that you won't be able to tackle what is emerging. This causes you to block out potentially unsettling information which reduces your understanding of the situation.

2. The negative feedback generates a negative emotional state which literally closes your creative mind and distorts your awareness of the choices and resources available to correct the mismatch.

As things escalate, the disengagement intensifies the physiological stress response. We become distressed where this accelerates and we head toward damage.

We Can Experience All Levels During the Day

You can use one of the "four ds" to describe your overall state. However, depending on your state of mind (desire), and available resources and skill level (capacity), you will experience varying levels of negative stress during the day.

For example, you may experience disengagement during a difficult commute, spend the morning doing great work and be on the positive spectrum and then have a difficult meeting that generates distress. So, instead of looking for "your position," look trends and patterns. These trends and patterns can determine your consistent or habitual experience and affect your ability to secure the resources you need to handle future stress. That is why our most frequent experiences can begin to create self-reinforcing patterns.

As a rule, you want to minimise the time you spend in these negative states. However, if stress is inevitable and is likely to increase over time, you need to change your relationship with it. How do you do that? I'm glad you asked!

How Can We Apply This?

To thrive in our new reality, we can embrace the wisdom of German philosopher Friedrich Nietzsche. He said:

"What does not kill me makes me stronger."[14]

Of course, it would be easy for us to challenge this and offer what on the surface could be equally true:

"What does not kill me may scar, traumatise, and maim me for the rest of my life."

This isn't as positive a message as the original and I think it fails to appreciate what Nietzsche meant. Nietzsche argued that we need difficulty and challenge in our lives to reach our best. Embracing challenge is the only real way we can overcome our perceived or actual limits. We can endure hardship, difficulty, and challenge and be strengthened by the experience.

So what does this have to do with having less stress and more success? We will be able to handle much higher levels of stress if we do two things: 1) increase our desire by choosing or accepting our short term stress, recognize it is happening and that we can and must tackle it; and 2) build capacity by ensuring the effect of our stressors help us to increase our strength and our strengths which will increase our ability to win tomorrow. In summary, we should strive to have the problems we have always wanted!

Strive for the Problems You Have Always Wanted

This clearly does not sound as attractive as the fantasy of being on easy street and having no more problems. However, you can actually achieve this and it's more fun than wasting your life sitting on a beach.[15] The problems you have always wanted should lead to stress you deem meaningful because it will either be an unavoidable cost of achieving your goals or it will help you to win tomorrow.

So you need to be more structured and deliberate about the distress you experience. If you think about it, this is not a new concept. Learning or doing anything significant involves challenge and stress. You have got to where you are today by choosing to be distressed. In sport, this is called *training* or *working out*; in business and the rest of society, it's called *learning*.

The answer to dissolving sustained workplace stress is not deep breathing or meditation—it's achieving mastery through focus, engagement, and capacity building. If you can find a meaningful goal you can't currently achieve and figure out how to do it, you will be well on the way to getting the problems you have always wanted. If you do this often enough and for long enough you will find yourself with problems you find absolutely fascinating that only you can solve. Other people may think you are crazy but you will be stressed, stimulated, and loving almost every minute.

How does this performance cycle model contrast the negative stress model?

Figure 2. The Performance Cycle

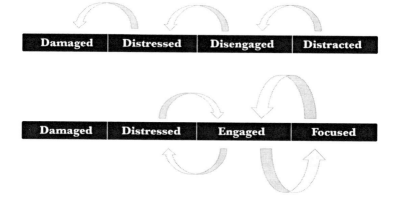

Feel Distress-Constructively and Strategically

Top performers oscillate most between engaged and focused. The better they are at delivering today's priorities, the more resources they have available to invest in tomorrow. They consciously experience distress by taking on challenges that are too much. This facilitates growth and helps them to win again in the next "round." To return to the training analogy if we aren't failing in some way, we won't be able to get the growth that comes from *safely* tearing the muscle and giving it time to recover.

So when you review the distress you and your organisation are facing, it will be important to ask "*For what?...What's the gain?*" If there isn't enough for you or those you care about, then you need to find ways to either reduce or eliminate it. This will release resources for faster recovery and better performance today and tomorrow. It is amazing just how much energy you can release by eliminating the stress that delivers nothing for your long-term growth and development. This is stress that used to serve a purpose but longer offers sufficient reward to be worthwhile. Far too many of us simply react to the momentum in a situation and forget to ask how this is going to serve our purpose. Taking control of your choice and asking the purpose question requires energy. Our first job will be to make this energy available by reducing what you have to spend to win today.

A Word on Damage

Sometimes people still move from distress to damage. It's inevitable as we sometimes stretch too far. Professional athletes recognize that damage (or injury) is an inevitable part of living on the edge of their capabilities. This isn't a reason to feel shame or inadequacy; it's a reason to review what you were doing, find out why, and introduce new measures to minimize the chance of that happening again. Therefore, how athletes recover effectively and plan their training to protect themselves more effectively tomorrow is perhaps the most important part of being a professional. Getting injured or making a mistake is fine: just ensure that the risks are worthwhile, that you can recover from the damage and use the learning to be stronger tomorrow. Do you have a strategy for that?

Becoming Isolated: Suffering Damage

Most damage occurs when you become isolated from your environment. You begin to ignore essential feedback which widens the mismatch and increases your challenge. You also neglect and even turn away from your support network which reduces both capacity and desire. Highly stressful situations cause you to focus on the task at hand and filter out what you see to be unnecessary stressors that are safe to ignore. Most of us see other people as additional sources of trouble instead of allies. Unfortunately, as the challenge grows, it becomes too much to handle on your own and the complexity goes beyond your individual understanding. We really could do with those allies.

Stress leadership is really an interactive team sport. If you haven't people around you that you can trust when the stakes are high, you will never be able to deliver exceptional performance for any sustained period. *Your environment will be high pressure, not high performance.*

When times are less stressed look at how you can improve the quality of interaction with your potential allies and with the environment in general. Alliances can save your life (both metaphorically and literally) and, according to the Art of War, the ancient military text, they are the second most important factor to focus on (after strategy). To increase your success here, begin by inviting help and collaboration when you don't need it. This gives you the time to tackle any relational friction so that everyone is aligned when the storm hits.

Help People Fail Forward

Going back to your position on the spectrum and the position of your people (if you lead), how clear are you on just how much distress you and your people are experiencing? As leaders, we ought to be encouraging our people to talk about areas they find challenging and to actively seek manageable and desirable distress. Consequently, we should actually be concerned if our people are not having distress in their work and projects. You want to know if anyone could be getting into trouble soon, but you also want to know that their efforts are worthwhile. This is the source of tomorrow's competitiveness, so it's essential it gets leadership time. How does the distress you and your people face develop the skills you need to succeed tomorrow?

Encouraging the right types of distress makes it easier for employees to speak out and ask for help when they are not being strategic in their distress choice. They also need to feel safe enough to speak if they think and feel they may be experiencing too much distress.

Consider your conversations with your people, how openly do they share their problems? How often do they ask for your perspective on the challenges they are facing and how hard they are finding things? Or do they spend most of the time persuading you they are doing brilliantly afraid to admit they find things hard?

Are you working in ways that protect you from injury–either actual physical injury or professional injury? I don't mean merely covering your back; I'm talking about structuring the more challenging and risky activities in such a way that failing to achieve can still lead to positive outcomes from the learning or momentum it generates. In other words, in what ways are you helping you and your people to fail forward? As a leader, how you deal with loss or failure makes an enormous difference to your long-term success.

I took up triathlon as part of my recovery and after an encouraging first year employed a coach. When we started working together, Annie Emmerson, a former World number 1, wanted to know about any niggles, aches, and pains I had before setting the training schedule. This allowed her to gauge the stress I was under and what my body could handle. It also taught me what pain I could ignore (because it was merely part of becoming a better athlete) and what I needed to pay attention to (the kind that could lead to injury).

Thinking about what Warren Buffet said in Chapter 1 about handling the basics and avoiding diversions, helping your people decide what they can safely ignore (figuring out what is a distraction or diversion) is a crucial activity. Most managers are unaware that it is one of the most useful things they can do with their people. An interactive feedback process such as the one I had with Annie minimised the chance of damage. Few managers are that focused on their people's performance or even able to engage at such a detailed, open level.

Confusing High Pressure and High Performance

High performance is not necessarily determined by the company that is currently winning in the market place. The leading team may be nowhere near their current potential. Most employees are working extremely hard in isolation but are wasting a great deal of energy doing things that should be done collectively. They rarely experience high performance. In the next chapter I will look at environmental factors that generate sustainable, high performance. This will help you to make a clearer distinction between high pressure environments and high performance environments.

Summary

- Stress occurs when there is a mismatch between the immediate demands of our environment and our ability or desire to adapt and recover.

- Our experience of stress (either positive or negative) is based on the degree to which we believe we are making progress (or winning) in an area we find meaningful.

- Our environment is too VUCA [volatile, uncertain, complex and ambiguous] for us to meet demands perfectly so some stress is inevitable. We can see stress as feedback on how well we are interacting with our environment and on our chosen strategies.

- Negative stress varies in intensity ranging from distraction to damage. As elimination of stress is impossible, it is essential to choose the types of distress that will help improve our ability to win in the future.

- Work to ensure the stress you experience is either unavoidable or constructive.

- To give us the resources to fuel our recovery and to win tomorrow we need to improve today's performance through increasing levels of engagement and focus.

- Isolation from our environment and our allies makes any stressful situation much worse. Dynamic interaction is the antidote to this.

- It is also important to stop assuming that your environment is benign and that anything you can do or see lots of people doing is safe. Whatever you choose to do, assess the risks and take full responsibility for the consequences.

- Given all the distractions that we face, one vital skill is to figure out what we can safely ignore.

- There is a big difference between high pressure and high performance. Most people are experiencing the former and confusing it with the latter.

3.
High Performance
Environments

Historically, a *safe* environment has always looked like a *stable* environment. Donald Schon, in the classic 1971 work, *Beyond the Stable State,* showed how we choose to believe in some kind of stable state to give us a sense of security. This sense of security reduces anxiety and helps us to function effectively in our environment.[16]

This is a delusion of sorts. Most of the time, it is a helpful and constructive one as it allows us to focus on the matter in hand and avoid being distracted—as long as we choose the right things to ignore. These are slower moving elements in our environment that have no relevant impact on our environment.

Dr Stephen Porges, director of the Brain-Body Center at the University of Illinois at Chicago, has done some stunning work into the importance and impact of having a safe social environment. According to Porges, if we don't feel safe we literally cannot access the parts of our brain responsible for creativity and collaboration and cannot perform at our best. For me, this work offers some tantalizing evidence why so many companies perform so far below their potential—their people are don't feel safe enough to stretch.

Porges' research into social environments deepens Schon's insight. This leaves us with an important question: *how can we create an essential sense of stability and safety when so many critical variables in our environment seem to be in flux?*

Feeling Safe in Turbulent Environments

This could be a tough question for us to answer. You can't control the level of challenge a business faces. You can't stop Chinese, Indian or German firms competing. So what can you do? Fortunately, the military, and other high stakes performers have some ideas on this. They find ways to feel safe enough to deliver excellence in often lethal situations.

Leadership in Dangerous Situations

A fascinating book, *Leadership in Dangerous Situations,* edited by three extraordinary leadership experts who worked together at the US Military Academy, West Point, (Colonel Pat Sweeney, Professor Mike Matthews and Captain Paul Lester) brings together some of the most up to date research available into leading in dangerous situations.[17] Their research (and experience) show that when lives are on the line, success depends on such things as trust, morale, resilience, ethics, decision making, cultural awareness, recruitment and development. When things *must* be right first time, you have to have already dealt with what is popularly known as "*the soft stuff.*"

Building a Safe Culture

If you want to make a turbulent situation feel safe, you have to create a sense of safety around your people. It has to exist not just in your building or organizational structure but in the relationships you as the leader have with each team member and in their relationships with each other. Relational fabric is the only one with the strength, flexibility and resilience to handle the most intense levels of stress. People will actively embrace appropriately distressing experiences if they trust and value the people around them and if they find the goal meaningful (which takes us back to the *Progress Principle*). The research also shows that the integrity of the leader forms an enormous part of this relational fabric.

My friend, US Marine Corp Lt. Colonel Mike Grice (Ret.), never had trouble sleeping in Afghanistan. He was able to handle the "*sporty*" or "*highly kinetic*" environment (euphemisms for being repeatedly shot at) because he was extremely well prepared for the challenges he faced. He was also surrounded by others who were equally prepared and committed. He could (and did) entrust his life with those people. They had the same values and the USMC knows values development is often the difference between winning and losing. It's the cohesion and skill generated by shared values and shared ways of seeing that allows seemingly telepathic actions between colleagues.

Mike, or any Marine in his command, didn't need to wonder if his or her colleagues would be supporting them: they knew. They were part of an extremely cohesive group of people who were willing to die for each other. In Porges' language, they had a safe social environment. The relational fabric was immensely strong. [And having been with Mike when he was reunited with some of the men he served with, this fabric seems strong enough to hold even if they don't see each other for months or years.]

One measure of a safe environment for Porges is that the colleagues can hug each other.[18] This seems to be routine in the USMC but is an amazing or even impossible standard in most high pressure business organisations where a lack of care for each other is often fostered by intense internal competition. One anecdotal cultural measure I help companies work towards is to create an environment where someone can make a mistake and know that it won't be used against them.

If you can go all out working to achieve individual and team goals without worrying about yourself and if you will be treated fairly, you will have a chance to commit sufficient resources to achieve your highest performance. To use a colloquial term, when you feel someone "*has your back*" at work, you will be able to give your best.

The Value of Values

In most organisations, values development was a nice to have even before the crash. Now it's hardly mentioned. But it's crucial if you want high performance. In dynamic environments, it's impossible to prepare for every possible scenario so you have to develop shared ways of working, thinking and behaving. This means that even if team members can't be sure what their colleagues are going to do in a new situation, they know they'll be supporting each other.

Values can give you both certainty and flexibility. There is nothing magical or mystical about them really. Values are simply the description of the most frequently used and rewarded behaviours in that organisation or team. It is possible to assess how successful those behaviours are in creating a match with the demands of that commercial environment. If appropriate, you can encourage other values and behaviours that would generate more long term benefits for the individuals and their organisations.

Values such as integrity, openness and trust may not seem to be directly linked with performance. They are probably the most important as they help people know what they can rely on. Being certain of some things means you can ignore them and focus on delivering. For example, knowing how an appraisal system works in the organisation and that it has a ruthless commitment to fairness means a top performer can stop worrying if they will be treated equitably. Having a leader who is trusted means everyone can focus externally as the trusted leader will protect them from trouble within the company. It's this focus on key values that can create a sense of safety even in organizations experiencing massive change.

The Difference That Makes a Difference

There are a number of ways to tell if you are in or if you have created a high-performance culture. One is to simply look at the patterns distress everyone is experiencing. Is the stress individual, i.e. is it a problem with a few of your staff? Or is it more ingrained and general—a problem that most people experience?

Deming, one of the greatest management thinkers of the last century, suggested that if 10% of your people are having a problem, assume it has a special (or specific) cause—i.e. *they* need help. But if far more people are having the same problem it's more likely that the system or structure needs attention as it has a common (general) cause. The more you have common problems, the less likely it is that you will have high performance.

Because leaders usually spend too little time developing the relational fabric in the organisation, employees have to do for themselves what should be taken care of by the firm. They have to figure out whom to trust, fight to be treated fairly, and protect themselves from internal attack. To give you an analogy from my property work, working in a company with weak relational fabric is like being asked to paint a room as you hold up the ceiling.

In many organisations, employee stress is often caused by corporate strategies and structures failing to reflect the changing realities of the market place. If there is reluctance from senior management to engage on the common causes of stress in your organisation, you will need to create your own support network to help you deal with it yourself. This isn't a long-term solution but it can protect you from short-term harm. As this is beyond our 90-day focus, this is something to consider over the next year. What I will say is that there is often far more flexibility in these situations for a proactive, resourceful leader. If you focus not on changing the company but adapting to your specific situation, you are likely to make more progress. In effect, you create a safe micro-environment.

How much trust is there between your team members? How safe do you or they feel to strive for challenging goals without having to check for problems or threats? Can you make an honest mistake, be rewarded for the effort, and then helped to ensure that you recoup the losses next time through your improved awareness of what works?

Having the Time and Resources to Adapt

All the teams studied in *Dangerous Situations* handled the intense time pressure of the crisis through extraordinary preparation. They recognized that stress is not simply a matter of the challenge exceeding resources (either perceived or actual). With learning, capacity building, and innovation you can often get far more from the same resources. Anticipation allows you to move resources from one part of the business (or your life) to another.

The "*immediate demands*" in the explanation of stress could refer to any time frame. How much time you have depends on your preparation, the speed and force of the feedback you receive and the resources you have for recovery. Sometimes, "*immediate*" can be a moment, other times it's a number of years.

The word "*crisis*," at its Greek root, simply means "*to decide*." It's the speed and unpredictability of the situation that causes trouble. To achieve high performance, you need to influence the duration of "*immediate*". Simply the time you have to meet the demands in your environment, it needs to be long enough to give people a chance to learn from their experience and get another chance to reapply that learning. Creating the time to learn and reapply is a tough thing to do in a pressurized environment. But it can be done if you create the right culture.

Also, if time is scarce then you need to look for ways to spread the stress between a team of people. Given the teams can take time to develop, it's important that you prepare the team in advance. If you don't have that time, then each individual must trust the leader enough to feel safe with being fully stretched with a group of strangers. It's hard for a leader to create this bond with each individual so it must have happened before the mission or project begins. Each member needs to be able to trust that the person making the toughest decisions is someone who is qualified (both personally and professionally). This can happen if the organisation is small enough for each person to know that leader in some way. Or it can happen if each person trusts the organisation enough to know that the people in leadership positions have been selected for because of their performance and for no other reason such as nepotism or favoritism.

Plan First to the Horizon and then Beyond

When we face any situation, we take time to orient around what is happening. This helps us to make the right choices and also helps to provide reassurance that things are stable or safe enough for us to be OK. In turbulent environments, people can be so challenged by the speed and velocity of a change that they refuse to act until they have collected enough information to be certain that they are not making a mistake.

In stable or known situations, considering every piece of information that could be relevant can help you arrive at the *best* answer. Conventional schooling tends to inadvertently encourage this thinking. To help learners, boundaries are set around what is and is not considered relevant for an answer [the teachers tell you what you can ignore]. Students are encouraged to work diligently through all the sources to find the correct answer. One author compared this learning to completing a puzzle like a jigsaw. All the pieces are known, and success is putting them back together in the pre-determined pattern.

If schools didn't frame learning to some extent it would be easy to become overwhelmed. Where would you start if there were no boundaries? Most of us would quickly feel helpless with all the decisions we had to make simply to frame the question.

In turbulent environments not only is this *"puzzle solving"* approach unhelpful, it's impossible. It's impossible for a number of reasons. To begin with when you first encounter turbulence you will only be able to see some of the pieces to your solution. There will also be lots of other random pieces that are irrelevant to your work. As the situation evolves, more pieces will become available. If it was as simple as waiting for all the pieces, we would simply need to make sure we are able to wait long enough for everything to come together. It's not that simple. Irrelevant pieces will also emerge, often faster than the relevant ones. We need to find a faster way to deselect them than waiting to see how everything turns out.

Essentially, you need to do two things. Firstly, follow the military adage and plan to the horizon. This means you need to understand all you can about your environment and figure out your probable best course of action. Secondly, learn or adapt more rapidly, skilfully and cheaply by quickly testing your understanding. Once you have the results from these tests, you can reapply the learning and repeat the process.

If we can get to the edge of the situation's evolution, we can actually begin to shape our own pieces. If there is a competitive element in our endeavour, we can sometimes shape pieces that are impossible for our opponent to use without massive adaptation of their existing pieces. How can we thrive in this crazy world?

These two activities–planning to the horizon and fast testing/adaptation–will help you to discover which behaviours generate the rewards of a) a new piece (which helps you to see more clearly what is going on) or b) the chance to make your own unique piece that fits only your jigsaw.

So on the one hand there is a bucket load of additional "VUCA" to handle. This is stress inducing. However, the potential reward is that you get to shape the future. This can be immensely exciting and rewarding. At other times, this trade off doesn't seem to be worth the trouble. So we need to find a way through to the situations where the rewards are worth our sometimes herculean efforts.

How Far is the Horizon?

The answer to the question that is probably going round your head–"*Jonathan, how far is the horizon?*" is dependent our answers to two questions: 1. how well do you understand the immediate demands of your environment?; and 2. how severe are the penalties for any mismatches?

We will be looking at the first question in the next chapter so let me quickly address question two. This takes us back to creating a safe environment. To succeed in turbulent environments, you need to design and run small experiments to see what works today. Each experiment needs to be structured in such a way that you could lose your entire investment and still be able to continue so that you could reapply the learning.

This concept is well known to traders and has been developed by entrepreneurship expert Saras Sarasvathy. She calls it *affordable loss.*[19] You then repeat winning actions and invest more aggressively in those ideas that are rewarded by the environment. This gives you the chance to secure the immediate future and to then start to shape the environment as it emerges. This is the reward for taking the necessary risks to understand what is going on.

In turbulent environments, the future isn't pre–ordained, it's waiting for you to pick up a chisel and get to work creating a coherent and compelling narrative (or piece) that connects what you've already done, what's happening now, and how this could develop in the future. A great example of a company that does this is Amazon.com.

Amazon.com–Shaping Its Environment

Amazon.com transformed book selling by eliminating costly customer mismatches (out of stocks, cost of searching for out of print books, cost of travelling to a book store, etc.). Having performed this task better than anyone else, they have built a trusted relationship with their customers so they can sell less standardised items that people find riskier to buy online–clothes etc.

Also, they have reduced competitive friction as traditional book sellers are now selling their products– the Kindle, etc. You can win without fighting, to paraphrase the Sun Tzu's *The Art of War* (the ancient Chinese military text).

One of the most important things Amazon did, though, is to create an environment where the company was able to experiment quickly to find opportunities and then make longer-term investments. These investments helped them to meet immediate demands (find and deliver books faster and more cheaply) and also to have much larger wins in the future. They shaped the competitive landscape by setting industry standards and preventing other competitors grabbing the early explosive growth in ecommerce. Amazon infrastructure now powers most online commerce.

Jeff Bezos, speaking in *Wired Magazine* in November 2011[20] said:

> *Our first shareholder letter, in 1997, was entitled, "It's all about the long term." If everything you do needs to work on a three-year time horizon, then you're competing against a lot of people. But if you're willing to invest on a seven-year time horizon, you're now competing against a fraction of those people, because very few companies are willing to do that. Just by lengthening the time horizon, you can engage in endeavours that you could never otherwise pursue. At Amazon we like things to work in five to seven years. We're willing to plant seeds, let them grow—and we're very stubborn. We say we're stubborn on vision and flexible on details.*

Amazon's short cycle experimentation followed by much longer cycle investments has shaped e-commerce and how everyone does business on the internet. And their competitors are now their customers as most major companies are using Amazon technology to power their online businesses. Amazon is now making the jigsaw pieces. That's a great long term vision. As a question to consider in the months ahead, think about how you could invest in your skills today that make you indispensable to your organization in future.

Summary

- To perform at our best we need to feel safe. Safety has historically been synonymous with stability. A stable external environment is hard to find today so we need to find other internal solutions to create that sense of safety in more challenging external environments.

- Research suggests that strengthening and improving the social environment can transform our ability to deal with turbulence as it creates a safe environment that can adapt to what happens around it.

- Core values such as trust, care, integrity, and openness help someone feel safe, valued, and supported as they tackle even lethal challenges.

- Unfortunately, most organisations pay insufficient attention to the behavioural expression of these winning values. This needs to be corrected if an organisation wants to create a sustainable high performance culture for itself and its people.

- An unsupportive social environment can be a source of many of the stressors people experience. If more than 10% of employees are experiencing problems with something it is usually more profitable to make a companywide, strategic response instead of relying on individuals to find their own way.

- If your environment is not supportive enough for you to tackle the challenges you face, you have to take more personal responsibility for your own safety. Create your own micro–climate.

- Running short experiments will help you to comprehend the changes you are facing and to piece together what is happening or to even create your own pieces.

- You can emulate companies like Amazon who try out lots of ideas quickly and cheaply and then invest heavily in the winners so that they can shape the future environment to their advantage.

4.
Understanding Your Immediate Stress Response

In this chapter, we will take some time for you to understand your own response to stress and where you are on both the short-term and the long-term stress curves.

Wernher Von Braun, the rocket pioneer, was once quoted as saying: *"The universe is hostile only when you do not know its laws. To those who know and obey, the universe is friendly."*[21] This is resonates with how most of my turnaround clients have previously interacted with their environment and it was absolutely true for me before my crash. So what are the laws that govern your stress response and how can we reduce the apparent hostility in our environment?

Answers to this question will help us to:

- Anticipate and prepare more skilfully for challenges.
- Learn faster and more cheaply about what works in your environment.
- Recover faster and more deeply.

Before we go any further, let's revisit our definition of how stress–the price the body pays for dealing with stressors–is caused.

> *Stress occurs when there is a mismatch between the immediate demands of our environment and our capacity and desire to adapt and recover.*

I need to briefly explain the two "types" of stress we face. They are acute stress and chronic stress. I will then explore what impact they can have in turbulent environments if we do not address them in the right way. After that, I will invite you to review your own stress response and then look at what you can do to immediately reduce distress and increase eustress.

Acute Stress

Acute stress is a short-lived, yet intense, episode of stress. It is focused on an immediate demand or challenge and, once met, goes away. Depending on the intensity, the effect can be positive and can increase performance. Given its short duration (and with sufficient time to recover), acute stress rarely causes long-term damage.

Assessing the Impact of a Stressor

The impact of a stressor depends on a few factors.[22] You can use this list of factors to determine how challenging something is going to be and how hard it will be for you to deliver expert performance. The first two are most obvious and relate to the challenge side of the basic stress equation. These are **severity** and **duration**. The other key element (which relates to resources) is the **recovery time/support** (internal and external) that is available before and after the event.

The final factor can reduce both desire and capacity. Previous **maladaptation** to stressful situations, such previous trauma, mental health issues and alcohol or substance abuse, can impair an individual's ability to perform.

We Need Some Stress–but Not Too Much

Acute stress was the initial focus for early stress researchers. Two pioneering psychologists, Robert Yerkes and John Dodson, proved that stress was essential for performance.[23] With insufficient arousal, people tend to be uninterested and disengaged and performance is low. As stress increases so does performance–to a point. Eventually, someone reaches their positive maximum and the stress begins to impair thinking and performance. This research produced the most famous graph in the field of stress research, the Yerkes-Dodson stress curve, which I have adapted in Figure 3.

Figure 3. The Adapted Yerkes-Dodson Curve

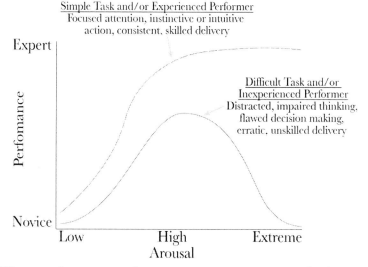

The performance drop is most pronounced for inexperienced performers with a complex task. This represents the greatest mismatch between the demands of the environment and the capacity and willingness of the performer. By contrast, a simple, engaging task (shown by the dotted line) has a much smaller mismatch (and mostly in favour of the performer). Because the task is simple, they don't require such high levels of thinking.

Consequently, performance levels can remain high for much longer than for the difficult task and/or the inexperienced performer. Whether something is simple or difficult depends on the performer's ability and the strategies or processes they use to achieve the task. If you are highly capable and experienced with robust processes, you will make a difficult task simple. Consequently, you will be able to maintain expert performance for longer even under intense stress. If your performance is impaired in some way, perhaps through tiredness, injury, distraction, or other forms of stress, your experience and skill could count for little and you may perform like a novice.

You Need Old Habits in New Situations

The behaviours you need in the tough situation must be habitual and deeply ingrained if you want to deliver expert performance. Experts keep things simple and get safely through difficult situations. Novices don't. As stress increases, we tend to fall back on our deepest habits or instinctive behaviours. Colonel Mike Wyly USMC (Ret.) helped rewrite US Marine Corp doctrine and did as much as anyone to improve the education and training of Marines in the post–Vietnam era. Here is what he has to say about the importance of habits:

> The habits you form in training are the habits you're still going to have when you are under pressure. And when you are under pressure you are going to go back to the familiar whether you like it or not. I have seen men throw away their lives because they wouldn't believe me when I said it doesn't get any easier when you have someone shooting back at you.[24]

I work with my clients to develop habits that are strong enough to tackle extreme situations. One reason why they get such improvements is that we ensure that they practice and use these habits in normal situations.

When you are reviewing the behaviours you need in important situations, look for ways to use them every day. All expert performance comes from intense, repetitive practice of simple actions. The better you are at practicing and honing these behaviours, the more stress you will be able to handle. Thinking you can deliver when it matters when you haven't developed the fundamental skills is utter delusion. Success takes intense practice and simplification. We will be looking at ways to do this later in this chapter.

Acute stress is the first type of stress. I've said it rarely does us harm, so what's the fuss about being more stressed? This brings us to the second type of stress and this is the one that leads to nearly all of our problems. This is chronic stress.

Chronic Stress

Originally, chronic stress described less severe but long lasting stressors such as persistent financial worries, family illness, etc. from which there was little chance for recovery. These could last months or years. Chronic stress is the type that leads to long-term illnesses such as high blood pressure, diabetes, and heart disease.

Most significantly for us today, the cause of most chronic stress has evolved and it's in this evolution that we have our biggest problems.

The Evolution of Chronic Stress

Today, people typically become chronically stressed for different reasons to the ones 50 or even 15 years ago.

Instead of low level, persistent stressors mentioned above, chronic stress is more frequently caused by a chain of acutely stressful events, that is, short, severe events that come too close together to permit sufficient recovery. Having made only a partial recovery, your base arousal level rises a little for each successive experience. This makes each successive stressor a little more challenging as it is building on the cumulative effects of all those partial recoveries. Eventually, we find ourselves blowing up over the smallest addition challenge. It's the proverbial "*straw that broke the camel's back*." To be clear, it wasn't the straw's fault but the fact that you never got rid of previous loads.

This makes today's stressful environment **intense** (like acute stress), **long lasting** (like chronic stress) and so turbulent we are **unable to recover**. That's all three of the most common factors for determining how hard a stressful experience will be. Is there any wonder why there are so many people suffering with stress.

Swank and Marchand–The Effects of Chronic Stress

During the Second World War, two doctors, Roy Swank and Walter Marchand, studied the effects of prolonged combat on soldiers entering France on D-Day.[25] (Imagine them following Tom Hanks' unit in "*Saving Private Ryan*"). They published their study in 1946.

Figure 4 shows the effects prolonged combat had on performance. This is perfect for our work because the soldiers didn't face one single acutely stressful event. They endured a chain of intense engagements with insufficient time between for a full recovery. That's why their stress curves increased.

Soldiers had what can euphemistically be described as *"an intense learning experience"* in the first five days followed by a dramatic increase in performance. They reached their peak between Days 10 to 12. On average, the soldiers maintained this level of performance until they started to decline around Day 20.

Figure 4. The Effects of Chronic Stress

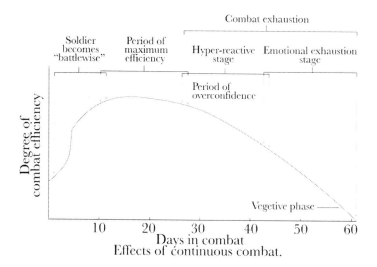

Effects of continuous combat.

The shift from maximum efficiency to combat exhaustion also shows one of the most pernicious aspects of negative stress–you don't realize you are in trouble until it is too late. This over-confidence causes someone to stop paying attention to their experience which prevents rapid adaptation and recovery. The deterioration is noticed later–and then usually by others.

Finally, this research showed that after 60 days of continuous combat almost everyone (98%) developed psychological problems. Those who didn't had what the authors described as "*aggressive psychopathic personalities.*" (In other words, they were crazy already.)

Another outstanding author, Lt Colonel Dave Grossman US Army (Ret.), compared this research with the actions of the British military in World War I. They believed soldiers could fight safely for hundreds of days before suffering similar effects. Grossman suggests that the difference was that the British rotated soldiers away from the front lines every 12 days for four days of recovery.[26] This approach gave soldiers a chance to recover, which would have taken their stress levels down and made the stress acute instead of acutely chronic.

One of the benefits of the relatively static nature of the First World War (at least from a stress perspective) was that there was a much clearer distinction between areas that were deemed safe and those deemed unsafe. Linking this back to Porges' work, this safety would have allowed soldiers to relax enough to recover. With the current conflicts in Afghanistan and Iraq, it is impossible to define a "*safe area*" due to presence of IEDs and the infiltration by enemy forces of groups defined officially as "*allies.*" The extra vigilance this demands from troops makes it extremely difficult for them to relax enough to allow their bodies to recover fully.

Bringing this back to my corporate work, many executives facing intense workplace stress/conflict often neglect their families in an attempt to get the job done. This can lead to conflict at home as family members are understandably upset at not being a priority. This home conflict means the executive is unable to relax and recover sufficiently to be able to sustain their excessive output/energy expenditure.

Consequently, I now look to help people improve their home lives as well as their work performance. Often this is the first thing that we do. I appreciate the seemingly contradictory nature of this–someone is facing overwhelm at work so I encourage them to spend more time at home. However, without a safe, supportive home environment, how can there be any recovery?

Severity is Not Your Problem

To summarise, with acutely stressful events, we need to focus on severity and duration (with an assumption we'll get to recover soon). However, now that our acute stressors come so closely packed together, we can no longer do whatever it takes confident we can make it up during the recovery phase.

To get through today's version of chronic stress, we need to pay much more attention to recovery and support. Ignoring recovery is where the damage is done.

Experience, endure, recover, and come back stronger is our goal. Far too often we experience, endure, partially recover, and come back a tiny bit weaker. This puts on an accelerating collision course with something hard and unforgiving.

The most dangerous thing is that the second pattern is indistinguishable to the healthy pattern in the short term. So someone can look at the impact their stress is having and conclude, "*So far, so good!*" They need to be looking more closely and over a longer time frame where they can determine impact their actions are having on future capacity. Are they really flying or do they need to be worried about which floor they are passing through like the man in the first story in this book?

On this cheerful note (sorry!), I'd like to pause so that we can summarise what we have covered. I promised that you would get chance to explore your own experience of stress and we will do that next. I promise whatever you find you are heading in the exercise we can change the speed and direction very quickly.

Summary

- Stress is essential for performance and is initially fun. So it's profitable to find ways to extend those positive effects through engagement, mastery and task simplification.

- We don't need too much stress to impair our performance if we are doing brain intensive (complex) tasks.

- If we can recover quickly and deeply enough, we can experience stressful situations without serious negative effects. Tough situations are rarely damaging if you get sufficient recovery.

- We often don't realise it when we have peaked. This makes self-awareness of where you are on your performance-stress curve important. With that awareness and insight, we can minimise trouble and dramatically reduce recovery time.

- If we have enough stress without enough time to recover, we all go crazy.

- Severity and duration are not the most important elements in assessing a stressor. Instead you need to focus more on duration and recovery.

Exercise

Take a few minutes to reflect on your experiences about the stresses you face [this can be done with a colleague or friend]. What combination of acute and chronic are they? What's their impact? How do you recover? When and where do you feel safe enough to relax?

The Stress Response: Understanding the Different Factors

We are now going to explore the current (mis)match between you and your environment in more detail. This exercise should take 20–60 minutes.

Please record your answers to in a note pad as we'll be coming back to your answers later.

1. What sources of positive and negative stress do you experience?
2. In what ways (physical, mental, emotional, etc.) do those stressors affect you?
3. On a scale of -10 to +10, give each stressor a score based on its effects for you (-10-0 for the negative ones and 0 to +10 for the positive ones.)
4. At what times and in what situations are you more likely to experience a) positive stressors? b) negative stressors?
5. Looking at this list, what patterns or groupings seem to emerge (this could be for stressors or for impacts also). What does this suggest?
6. If you were able to reduce or eliminate up to five of these negative stressors, which ones would represent the best investment of your time and energy? This could be the highest scoring ones, but you also need to consider the frequency and the timing of their impact. You may rate a poor response to some tough questions from your boss' boss as rare but so potentially damaging that this will be one you'd like to improve. Also, there may be some stressors that act as catalysts for longer stress reactions. So if you could stop the catalyst, you can prevent the whole response.

We are now going to explore your response to two to three different events that cause stress for you. This is best done if you have some specific events or stressors in mind.

1. Take 2-3 different events that can stimulate a prolonged stress response even though they may last only a few minutes—for example, road rage, a verbal fight with a colleague/partner/boss, etc.

Draw the stress curve for that individual event (with arousal on the vertical, time on the horizontal). The level of arousal is going to be largely subjective but be as precise as you can about the time. What does your stress curve look like? What is the build up? For how long before and how long after do you experience higher activation (arousal)?

Try to think about someone who doesn't seem to experience the level of activation you do before an event—what do they do that's the same/different from your behaviour? Speak to that person or observe him or her if you can. Ask the person about what he or she is thinking and feeling (and saying to him- or herself) as well as what he or she actually does. Reapply some of their ideas.

Do this for two to three of those events before moving on.

We'll come back to these answers at the end of this chapter. I'd like to focus on ways in which you can improve your acceleration and braking for single events. This will reduce the total cost of the stress you experience as it will reduce both the duration and severity of the acute stressors and create more resources for recovery.

4a.
Improved Acceleration and Braking

Our first focus of attention is the ways that our thoughts and feelings about the demands we face can affect our willingness and even our capacity to meet those demands. What's your answer to the following question?

What's the Biggest Cause of Stress – The Event or Your Response?

"Events, dear boy, Events." [27]

It's tempting to think the events do it to us. Harold MacMillan, UK Prime Minister in the late 1950s and early 1960s, seemed to think so when asked what he feared most as P.M. However, research shows that it's not the event stressor that damages, but our emotional response to that event. As Hans Selye said:

"...for man the most important stressors are emotional." [28]

Emotions are crucial to stress leadership. They provide instinctive and intuitive information about your environment and the challenges you are facing. The goal is not to suppress or ignore them but to ensure you have the right emotions at the right level at the right time. It is helpful to be more open to your emotional landscape and to develop your emotional intelligence. [EQ is your ability to recognise, understand, and constructively handle your emotions and respond to emotions of those around you.]

We gain more influence over our external environment and what happens to us if we can first improve our internal emotional response. This improved response ensures that the emotional energy we have in our bodies is at a level that will help us.

If we are unable to generate helpful emotional responses, we can get hooked onto a single stressful event. This actual event may last a few moments but the reaction it triggers could affect us for the rest of the day. For example, think of the last time someone cut you up in your car. This was a potentially life threatening event, so your body will have stimulated a stress response. If this lasts for a few seconds, you will have had improved reflexes and enhanced focus. The acceleration helped us to respond skilfully. However, if you were unable to put on the emotional brakes and return to normal levels of activation once the threat had ended, you could have been affected for hours as you ruminated over what happened or what could have happened. This increases our vulnerability to another acute stressor triggering a chronic stress response.

To be clear, board meetings do not need to become group therapy. Can you imagine a USMC platoon commander asking his men how they feel when they are under fire? But what we do need to do in organisations is to end the delusion that you can operate in turbulent environments and ignore the inevitable and essential emotional responses and reactions. Emotions enable the right responses if they are the right emotions. If we can accept the inevitability and the vital nature of emotions we can work to ensure we experience emotions that help us to perform.

The good news is that this acceptance makes it possible for us to develop the ability to accelerate to meet a challenge and then quickly return to a calm, relaxed state of preparedness. This can lead to as much as a 95% drop in some forms of distress. We can do this if we can build the internal emotional mastery to be able to respond to what we experience instead of reacting and the professional mastery to address the mismatch that causes our stress.

To get some ideas on how to cultivate this mastery, we are going ask some 1970s Norwegian paratroopers for help. I know, those Norwegian paratroopers, who can do without them! Well, trust me, the theory and applications are brilliant. Before that, however, I want to give you a picture of what I mean by emotional and professional mastery. The story involves one incredibly well prepared team and a flock of errant geese.

The Greatest Benefits of Emotional Intelligence

Surprisingly, the biggest corporate benefit of promoting EQ is not happier employees. The greater your emotional mastery the more reality you can handle so you are less likely to ignore unsettling data or nasty surprises. You will be more willing to explore what is really going on which makes it possible for you to understand your environment much more accurately and insightfully. EQ allows you to think more clearly as your decisions can be aided by situationally appropriate emotions, instead of being clouded by unhelpful ones. All this leads to much better decisions and more skilful actions. In short, a higher EQ means *you will be less emotional!*

I know–It surprised me too! As amazing as this sounds, this is what the studies I've read say about people who thrive in high–stakes environments.

Example–Landing on the Hudson River

One of the biggest surprises of my research is that there is an absence of extreme emotion in extreme situations for those who are prepared. Captain "Sully" Sullenberger, with his first officer Jeff Skiles, safely landed a passenger aircraft on the Hudson River in January 2009 after both engines were hit by geese.

A chapter in his autobiography, *Highest Purpose*, describes the actual landing (wittily entitled "*Gravity*"). Sully speaks movingly of the passengers preparing themselves for death. Some were holding hands, others were writing loving notes on business cards in the hope that their final thoughts would reach their families after their death.

It was totally different in the cockpit. This is what was going through Sully's mind:[29]

> "*I did not think I was going to die…Lorrie, Kate and Kelly [his wife and daughters] did not come into my head either. I think that was for the best. It was vital that I be focused, and that I allow myself no distractions. My consciousness existed solely to control the flight path.*"

His autobiography shows a leader who spent a lifetime developing true mastery, serving others and preparing for greater challenges even when no one else seemed interested in offering them. Sully offers an amazing example of how to cultivate emotional mastery and professional brilliance.

We'll come back to some other insights from Sully later. Now, let's get back to those helpful Norwegians.

Lessons from Norwegian Paratroopers

The study we are about to explore is one of the best I have ever seen. It was led by Holger Ursin, Eivind

Baade, and Seymour Levine and took place at the Norwegian Army Parachute Training School in the 1970s. It was the first systematic psychoendocrine research in this field and the first to demonstrate scientifically that "*psychological factors are often more important in influencing certain outcomes than the physical stimuli themselves.*"[30]

The research team followed trainee paratroopers on their journey from novice jumper to expert. During that time they compared all the key stress measures available at the time. This was the first time this had ever been done. The research team found that novice jumpers had a fully activated physiology, including elevated heart rate and strong emotions for hours before the jump and remained for hours afterwards.

In contrast, once they had become proficient, they were calm and relaxed in the hours before and after the jump. Interestingly, they had even higher levels of activation just before the jump than they did as novices. This activation seemed to generate the ideal state of intense concentration and alertness needed to safely tackle the challenge of jumping from an aircraft.

In summary, as novices, the troopers had approximately eight to 10 hours of stress and strong emotional responses versus approximately 30 minutes as experts. The study clearly showed that the more suitably prepared you are, the less stress you will experience before and after an event.

Differences in The Stress Curves of Inexperienced to Experienced Performers

Let's take this back to our stress curve work. To make this easier (and more useful) let's move away from having performance–arousal axes and instead explore the links between arousal over time. In addition to making things clearer, this format also acknowledges the potentially complex relationship between arousal and performance. This will help us to see the opportunity for longer recoveries if we can respond more appropriately to single, acute stressors.

Let's place arousal on the vertical axis and time on the horizontal and look at the graphic difference between experienced and inexperienced performers.

Figure 5. Activation for Experienced and Inexperienced Performer

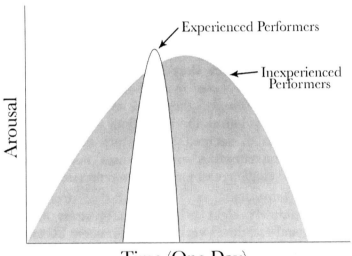

Remember, the experienced paratroopers were able to change the relationship between arousal and performance. They had less stress and higher performance but were able to get more highly activated than the inexperienced jumpers when it mattered (and when it helped them). We are looking to do the same for you. As you become more skilled at handling challenging situations, you can reduce the need for an external shock to generate performance and choose our own desired performance whenever you like.

Phasic vs. Tonic Activation

The type of activation you are working toward is something called *phasic activation*. This involves higher levels of adrenalin and an elevated heart rate. It improves focus, concentration, and alertness and lasts a few minutes when the adrenalin is used up. Phasic activation helps you to deliver. Even as the paratroopers became experts, they never stopped experiencing it. This suggests to me that it was an appropriate adaptation for jumping out of an aircraft.

The activation we want to minimise is *tonic activation*. This is slower to emerge and much longer lasting and is largely driven by cortisol, the stress hormone that in our world does all the damage to our health.[31] This is essentially how we turn acute situations into chronic ones and it was the key difference between the troopers when they were experienced (had hardly any unnecessary stress) and inexperienced (had hours of it).

"Just the Stress, Thanks!"

To paraphrase the famous TV cop, Sgt Joe Friday from the classic show Dragnet, instead of *"Just the facts, Ma'am,"* you'll dramatically reduce the impact of stressful situations when you can say *"Just the stress, thanks."* Find a way to remain alert yet calm before an event, respond most actively just before it occurs so that you are fully prepared, and quickly return to your previous state. This can reduce the experience of stress for my clients by as much as 95%. Aim to be *in* the situation but not *of* the situation.

At work, this strategy effectively turns a chronically stressful day into a relatively calm day with a few acutely stressful situations. You move from novice to expert.

Committing to choose your own response doesn't mean that you will be able to do this in every situation. Committing to do a triathlon for charity doesn't mean you will be able to immediately swim, bike, and run 70.3 miles. Sure, the intention or desire comes first but you then have to build the capacity through intelligent action, hard work, and commitment.

This is what we are going to focus on next looking at how we can apply the great research from Ursin, Baade and Levine. They have a lot to say about intelligent action, hard work and commitment.

How to Shrink Your Stress Curve

The research team highlighted a number of factors that influenced paratrooper stress levels. These are things you can consider if you want to reduce tonic activation and optimise phasic activation.

- One of the most fundamental findings is that stress increases if the event is perceived as threatening and/or uncertain. The first thing you can do is to build capacity through actively facing and mastering the situation. Greater skill and better preparation can make a 'high risk' event relatively safe. The event itself can be potentially life threatening but no more hazardous for an expert than crossing the road. Prepare, prepare, prepare.

- Two ways to increase your sense of safety and certainty come from applying the *preparatory response hypothesis*[32] (see the event coming so you can get ready) and the *safety-signal hypothesis* (create space/time where no further shocks are possible so that you can relax and focus on your recovery).[33]

-         Creating a safe space where no further shocks are allowed before the event allows you to focus fully on final preparation for the task. In sport, teams often have rules around making no further changes to the team or the initial plans or who is allowed into the changing rooms from a certain time before the event.

-         Improve the quality, quantity, and speed of the feedback you get. To thrive (or even just survive) in dynamic situations, it's essential you get feedback on your actions faster than the situation is emerging. In dynamic situations where there is little opportunity to reapply learning, most of this "feedback" on what works and what doesn't work often has to come in the practice and preparation phase. You then know what is most likely to work so you can minimise the need to think about new actions when the situation is developing quickly.

-         Professional service firms (PSFs) are tremendously fast moving, exciting environments. For the same reason, they are also potentially lethal (at least professionally). One of the most dangerous situations I see in PSFs is the delay that can take place between an event, someone's actions and highly consequential feedback that can impact future progression.

When working in these firms (or on fast moving projects), I look to introduce daily feedback sessions (or weekly sessions if the pressure is not as severe). Everyone quickly discusses what worked and what didn't that day/week so that everyone is a little better tomorrow and any mismatches are swiftly addressed. This helps everyone deal with the danger of developing unhelpful responses and not having the time to recover/adapt. If team feedback sessions are not possible, I will help my client to become more aware of the behavioural feedback available from how people are responding to their actions.

-        One reason why Sully brought everyone home safely was his ability to prioritise and sacrifice goals. He learnt how important this was from a career long interest into why air crashes occurred and what a pilot could have done to avoid them.

Pilots know that crashing a plane tends to be "career limiting." Sadly, to avoid this, some pilots work too long to recover a lost situation and fail to eject when they should. They lose their lives as well as the plane.

Sully's priorities were to keep the passengers safe and avoid damaging the aircraft. Once he realised he was unable to do both, he saved the passengers and sacrificed the "lesser" goal of saving a $130m plane.

If you want to be able to do this in a crisis, it's helpful to decide your priorities in advance. Then, the only real challenge is to ensure your behaviour remains consistent with that earlier decision.

-        Survival (physically or professionally) is the only real measure of success in some really tough situations. The paratrooper researchers found that the stress experienced by the trainees reduced dramatically when they felt they had "*performed*" (or made progress in Amabile and Kramer's language). Early in their training, this sense of progress had no link to actual performance. It was based purely on the trooper's self-assessment that they had a) survived and b) were less bad than last time, i.e. they were learning.

It's helpful to have modest expectations about first time performance in a dynamic environment, i.e. be happy you survived. Expecting excellence is likely to cause internal stress and interfere with performance.

-        Don't try to suppress emotions in tough situations. In the study, those jumpers who reported the highest (subjective) fear on their first jump from an aircraft performed more successfully (according to the instructor's evaluation) than those who suppressed their emotions and said they weren't that fearful. The research team found that a little bravado (delusion) can help overcome feelings of nerves or even fear in minor situations [for the paratroopers this was jumping from a tower]. However, bravado and emotional suppression will impair performance in serious situations [such as jumping out of a plane].

Instead of suppressing them, work to generate and experience the emotions that are relevant and appropriate. It is essential to admit your emotions at least to yourself. The honest jumpers were able to stop fighting their emotions and to find coping strategies to deal with them.

Trying to ignore something that is happening impairs your ability to focus on the emerging situation. You don't need to tell anyone else that you are feeling one thing or another as your higher level of emotional intelligence may be punished by less evolved colleagues. But you will be rewarded through improved performance if you are honest with yourself.

- The researchers make an excellent distinction between fear and anxiety. *"[F]ear is characterised by a clear and well defined threat stimulus. Anxiety is characterised by the absence of any such clear stimulus."*[34] So in a tough situation, the clearer you can be in naming your fear, the less difficulty you will have in tackling it. Go through the situation and write down your potential anxieties and get clear enough either to dispel them (because they were unfounded) or to turn them into defined fears. This may not sound like progress but it is. Once you know the challenge, you can figure out how to address it, either pre-emptively to through a better handled recovery.

-        Difficult situations were fine if the jumper enjoyed harmonious relationships with the people around them (work and home). Facing difficult situations with discord causes the most damage. We will touch on this in the Care and Support section.

-        "*The experienced jumper has a high fear level much earlier than the inexperienced jumper, and then fear and apprehension begin to decrease as soon as he reaches the airport and the maneuvers start.*" Many athletes look superstitious but few are. Most insist on doing the same things before games so they can stop thinking about what they are going to do. This helps them tackle what could easily be the unbearable stress of the situation. "*It may be crazy out there, and 1 billion people may be watching, but it's calm in here and I know what to do next.*" Their emotions tend to peak just before they go into the arena. The more things you can control before a big event without having to think about them, the more resources you will have left to prepare for your challenge.

Summary

I am going to complete the summary for this section by highlighting the most popular points my clients take from the paratrooper study in an exercise. This will help you increase your mastery over single (acutely stressful) events. Take one of the situations for which you drew a stress curve earlier and answer the following questions.

Questions for your Chosen event:

1. What's your level of mastery/experience? What previous experience have you got? If the situation is new, what's the closest thing you have experienced? What learning can you transfer from that situation to this one? How well can you predict what will happen in the situation?

2. If you are closer to novice than expert, who do you know who has been through this situation? What can they tell you about what to expect?

3. How can you rehearse the key challenges so that you can feel prepared?

4. What can you control in the situation? What can't you control? Who else will be "*on your side*" who may be able to control or influence these elements?

5. What else can you do to increase your level of mastery in this situation? What's the best you have ever been in this situation? What was it that caused your best performance? What were the most important factors? How could you replicate it again? What could you do to translate all this into a coherent strategy for winning?

6. What can you do to increase your consistency between your best performance, your average performance, and the performance you generated in that situation?

7. What's the potential downside in this situation? What are the anxiety inducing elements? How can you turn this anxiety into fear so that you can address them systematically? What's the lowest level of performance you will accept as success (e.g., surviving)? How realistic is this? [If you are demanding perfection the first time round then either change your expectations or accept that you will have to prepare far more than is worthwhile.]

8. How expensive would a loss be? To what extent can you afford it? If you can't, what can you do to make it "affordable," i.e. one from which you could recover? Which goals are you willing to sacrifice if you need to?

9. If you are preparing with others, agree when to stop taking in new information or changing decisions/

outputs. Sometimes the leader can make this impossible if they insist on keeping things open. If that happens, focus on what you and the rest of the team can do to be ready for last minute changes and to recover more rapidly.

10. What final preparation ritual can you create that you know will help you get into your top emotionally prepared state?

11. What feedback can you focus on during the event to ensure you stay on track? How about feedback on your stress state? Is there a level above which you will need to take a break? What can you do to ensure you get this break? This links with your emotional awareness and management. What can you do to ensure your emotions remain helpful for that situation?

12. What can you do to ensure that you have the most fun with this situation? You've got yourself into a challenging and exciting situation. This is a great opportunity to demonstrate your competence and become even better. Be sure to take a look around and enjoy the challenge.

13. What can you do to ensure you have time and space for appropriate recovery? What safety signal will tell you that it's safe for you to relax?

My clients write answers to most of these questions (and sometimes a few others) which we review and test. This increases confidence and sense of control as they head into the challenging situations—even ones over which they have little real control (such as separation conversations with their boss). What they can be sure of, though, is that regardless of their actual performance, they have put themselves in a position to do their absolute best.

In the next chapter, I will look at how you can fit these separate events together to make a good day or a good month. To do that, we need to look at how you spend your current resources and how you decide when it is safe for you to spend them.

5.
Your Resources: Costs, Spending and Replenishment

In the last chapter we were looking at ways to accelerate and brake more effectively. This will help you understand your stress and to cultivate an expert response to acutely stressful situations. This chapter is about reducing costs and ensuring you can keep spending or investing in areas that contribute to your future.

Some important questions to consider about what you are currently spending are:

- How and where are you spending your resources?

- How can you ensure you are spending only what you can afford?

- What can you do to eliminate unnecessary spending?

- How can you keep track of your resources and keep yourself fully resourced?

The chapter is split into three sections. The first section will help you to assess how much you are currently spending and what that spending is likely to cost you in the future. 5a offers some suggestions for reducing your spending and for spending more wisely on activities that will help you to win tomorrow. And 5b offers a more holistic way of viewing your resources and strengths. This will help you to you to get greater balance, faster replenishment, and more abundance going forward.

Resource Usage and Replenishment Check Exercise

This exercise will help you to:

- Know your current (over) spending
- Appreciate where the resources come from and how they are replenished
- Make clear your thoughts and assumptions about your resources so that you can test if they are true.

This exercise is based on your subjective assessment but is still worthwhile.

In your notebook, draw a table with four columns.

Column One–Make a list of all the key areas/activities of your life where you spend *time* and *energy*.

Column Two–Write down what percentage of your time and energy you give to that area (what it costs you). Feel free to make two columns. For some people time and energy are currently the same (they commit the same amount of energy as time). Other people vary the intensity of their time investment so some activities are time consuming but have relatively light energy requirements and others are fairly brief but exhausting.

Column Three–Write down what you get back– i.e., In what way does this area energise you (replenish or increase your resources)?

Column Four–Make an assessment as to whether this area is currently a net energiser or net sapper of your energy.

Take your time with this. It's a simple exercise but it can be hard to complete, especially when we have been investing/spending our resources in areas that are not our main priorities.

There's a lot of talk about how people have too much credit card debt. I see the same thinking with people taking too much energy debt – committing to things that require energy they really need for other areas. I frequently see leaders borrowing from their families to pay for their work. Now there is invariably a trade-off here as work is called work for a reason and work brings in financial resources. What's important is that this relationship works for all stakeholders and that any borrowing is agreed and repaid at some point.

One client was fully extended at work on a number of large transformation projects. He travelled extensively and was away from home at least three days in the week. Other than financial rewards, he could not think of any way his immediate work gave him replenishment. He had received no development, appreciation or positive feedback in more than two years. I asked him how he carried on and his reply was that he had a supportive family.

"So," I said, "your family is effectively investing in you so you can invest in work. How confident are you that your investors agree with this? You may want to clarify what they think of your choices. Make sure they are OK with what is going on. This will be good for your family but it will also protect the resources that are keeping you going through this transformation."

Using Stress Bands

Another way to illustrate your resource consumption or "burn rate" to use an old business term is to integrate it into your adapted stress curves.

You may remember that Hans Selye, the stress pioneer, said –that stress was *the rate of all the wear and tear caused by life*. Selye also suggested that we have a fixed amount of adaptive energy to pay for that wear and tear.

When we think about all the things our body does throughout the day, there are some fixed costs—the cost of keeping us standing up and our standard bodily functions and some tasks we have to do to fulfil our core responsibilities. It's rather like having to factor in things like rent, utility bills, food, etc. for our financial budget. For simplicity's sake, let's say you start off with a capacity of 100 units of adaptive energy and that you spend 50 of those units just to run all the systems you need to function.

Figure 6. The Different Levels of Stress

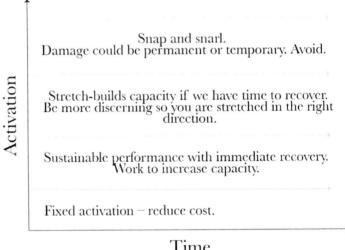

If you have 50 units in use, you have 50 available today for immediate spending. In addition to the base line, you can draw another line at 100 to show a level at which you can make an immediate recovery. If you wanted to keep things stable, you could continue until the environment changed and you had to change spending. However, as you are likely to want improvement, there will be times when you want to save resources, invest, or even bring spending forward to accelerate new skill development today.

The times when we invest are those times when we choose to be stretched and constructively distressed. This is performance that is achievable, rewarding, and safe if you have time to recover. Above that, there are more lines of challenge until you suffer damage. We can call that the S*nap line* for when you stretch too far. The greater the snap, the greater the pain, the longer it will take to recover.

Where Are Your Actual Lines?

Could you draw your own lines onto the adapted stress curves you drew earlier? Why don't you take a more detailed look at where it feels you have been operating for the last three months? On a graph, take some time to consider the fixed tasks from your list of activities how much of your available resources they use. Then, factor in everything else you are doing.

Are you at Sustaining, Stretch or Snap?

When you have done this ask:

What impact are my current actions having on my future capacity? That is, in what ways are they a) making me stronger b) making me weaker? (You may be neglecting core maintenance of yourself and or your relationships).What can I do about this?

Most people I work with have neglected future capacity investments as they have been challenged beyond their immediate capacity by current demands. Effectively they have been borrowing from tomorrow. If this doesn't result in increased capacity, it will reduce future capacity just as spending the capital from your savings account instead of just the interest will reduce your future earning power. You can do it for a while but you eventually run out of funds.

Using the Bands

There are some things you can do with your stress bands that can transform your response to stressful situations. We will look at those in the next section. For now, consider:

Get out of snap and snarl situations. You can do this in two ways. Firstly, ask what can you do to get yourself out of this situation as quickly and as safely as possible? This may take some time so do only what is essential and stop doing some things immediately (preferably with the agreement of your stakeholders.) As you plan your exit, increase your focus on signs of deterioration which could signal a collapse. If you see one coming then you may have to walk away [remember Sully's insights on goal sacrificing. Then make more of any recovery time and minimise any other stressors

The other option for dealing with Snap and Snarl is to increase your capacity by so much that the level becomes your new sustainable performance. This requires additional investment that you have to borrow from somewhere. If you can't afford my help (!) then find someone else to support you. I have never seen this done by someone working alone. That's not to say that it is impossible, just that I have never seen it so you had better be sure of what you are doing. Snapping hurts—a lot.

Review where you are stretching. Look at the areas where you are stretching. Check to see what skills and capabilities they are helping you to develop and how that fits with your view of the future. Are you being stretched in ways that will help you to win tomorrow? If not, look to change the areas where you are being stretched. It may be difficult to do things immediately but you will be able to make some changes in three months.

Increase your sustainable performance level. The higher your sustainable performance level the more you will be able to do without being stretched, the more you will have available for investments in future capacity.

Reduce your fixed costs. Look at what you have to do to simply deliver the basics and find ways to reduce your costs and conserve resources. This will make more adaptive energy available for delivering your performance today and tomorrow.

For all areas, look to abandon completely (stop doing) as many activities as you can. Merely reducing them postpones the tough strategic priority setting you are likely to need so much. If you do only what is essential, you will have less stress today and more energy to invest in the future.

The rest of the book will help you to achieve these outcomes. I will focus the rest of this chapter on how to make better use of the bands.

Improve The Quality of Your Data

One obvious potential problem with your assessment of where your bands really are is that you may not have any accurate data. How sure are you that your answers are accurate? What data do you have? How could you test it? I recommend you take some time reflecting on your experiences over the last two years (or as far back as you can remember). Look at your resource spend. What were you spending? What impact did that have?

At what times did you feel yourself getting stronger or more tired and weak? Were there times when you felt sure you would break but didn't? Any times when you felt sure you wouldn't break, but did? This is something that will take time but it is worth the effort. It gives you a much clearer idea of exactly where you are on your curves and what spending is safe to make. You need to find a way to safely explore your limits. Then spend the next few months paying much closer attention. One thing you can do is to actively test your limits.

Test Your Limits. Push Yourself to Failure

When I had lost my excess 70lb, I had a niggling worry that being so overweight and neglecting myself so badly may have done long-term damage. I found a sports testing laboratory and completed a series of test, including a Vo^2 Max test which is a fitness test where you run or cycle until failure whilst a doctor monitors all your vital signs.

The results from all the tests showed that I was completely fine, and that any fears I had were unfounded. As well feeling reassurance and relief, I became far more confident pushing myself in races or in training. I now knew what collapsing felt like (it wasn't so bad). Most helpfully, I knew what one minute before collapsing felt like. This gave me a much better early warning system for accurately gauging how much further I could push myself and still be safe.

If you are working in a supportive environment, you can safely take on more than you can handle to test your limits. Be sure to have a colleague look for the signs that you are get really stressed who could intervene if appropriate.

When starting out in my carcer at Procter & Gamble, I had a fantastic training manager called Steve Ashcroft. He was extremely good at using real sales meetings to develop my selling skills. If it got too challenging he would, if invited, step in. Other times he would let me flounder and I could take the learning.

Remember at all times, we are aiming for stretch and not snap so push but come back in one piece. As Saul Alinsky once said, "*The first rule of a revolutionary is to get away with it!*

Test Your Assumptions

Linked to testing your limits is to test your assumptions. When you spend any resources, you are assuming that you can afford the spending. However, few people ever think to check this assumption is still valid. Someone asks you for something, so you give it. My own experience has shown this is dangerous. It is the same as paying any bills or requests for charitable donations without knowing just how much is in your bank account.

When you are committing resources, answer the following questions:

1. What am I agreeing to do? What do I want to do?
2. How much will this cost and how will I pay for it? (Be sure to check how you know this)
3. How long will it take me to regain my balance and replenish these resources?

Record your answers for any meaningful resource investment for the next few months. Review how closely your assessment matched the actual cost and recovery time. Then reapply the learning in the next round. Simply underestimating how much things cost is one of the biggest reasons why we get into trouble. Most people who struggle with time management don't actually have a time management problem (poor organisation etc.) They actually have an "*assessment of how much time this will take*" problem.   If you simply ask how much something actually costs in terms of your resources and check if you have those resources, you will reduce dramatically the chance of getting into trouble I experienced.

5a
Ways to Reduce Costs and Speed up Your Recovery

Can You Really Have It All? N–O!

Pre-crash, I thought I could handle anything. I thought the metaphorical cupboard (me) would always be stocked regardless of my spending and what life threw at me. At least that's what I thought. Crazy, eh? How could I believe something so daft? Simple; I thought I had proof. For my first 35 years, I had always found a way whatever the challenge. So I never worried how I would find the resources to pay for something. I was certain the resources would come. A true abundance mentality! In my 36th year, the financial crash hit which changed the landscape dramatically. I was still unaware of this fundamental change (and that I was delusional) and so I ran full speed into the abyss.

I had a lot of time for reflection as I sat at the bottom of this rather large hole. I realised this delusion (of infinite resources) is everywhere. Most executives (and every turnaround client I have worked with) have that same secret belief they are infinitely resourced–most of the time it's so secret they don't realise they have it.

You Can't Be 100% All The Time

A variation of having it all is thinking you go all out all the time. Many businesspeople tell me they operate at their maximum all the time (stretch). This is possible in the short term (you can give more than 100% if you take your resources for recovery and maintenance) but is impossible to sustain. Stretch requires recovery time.

Also, if you want to spend time above the line, you need to spend time below it.

Operating at stretch all the time with insufficient rest simply lead either to Snap (if you really push) or to a gradual deterioration in performance of which you will be unaware. [This is just like the troops in the Swank and Marchand study].

You can delay this deterioration temporarily if you steal resources from other parts of your life (usually families and personal health). These are simply delaying and increasing the size of the inevitable crash when it comes. And it will. To get around this you need to be more strategic in your areas of focus and cut back. To do this, you need to accept a few more things. Choose what to focus on.

You are Breakable

I think being overcommitted both in resources and in expectations is one of the main reasons why so many of us feel such scarcity in a world of such abundance. It's a prevalent problem so there has to be some cultural blind spots that make our collective insanity so easy to do.

It's fun to believe we are limitless which may be why so many of us try to believe it. We also get lots of help from society too. Authors and marketers tell us you can have it all, you can live the life you see in commercials, do anything you want, and that opportunities/ resources/life are all unlimited! My favourite bit of nonsense is: "*Impossible is nothing*!"

These distorted perspectives (to be polite) look superficially inspiring but they are actually major sources of negative stress. Believing that anything is possible will increase your stress levels as they cause you to make impossible comparisons. They also suggest in a wonderfully perverse way, that if we haven't got it all, and if we are having trouble, it's really our fault. Anyone who believes that anything is possible who finds they *can't* do anything has to be to blame (if you follow the logic). If only we could find a different way, we would succeed! So the beliefs also encourage us to take on impossible challenges or take dangerous risks.

Bucket of cold water. You can't and won't go on forever. Impossible is simply impossible. Anything else is poor assessment or bad advertising. But here's the good news–accepting your limits will actually increase your confidence, satisfaction, and performance.[35] You can plan more confidently as you know where you need to stop to remain safe. You also can start being more ruthless with your choices in every part of your life without feeling guilty as you know you need to choose what's most important. And you realise that if you are committed to helping others, you must take care of yourself first–just as you need to put on your own gas mask on a plane before helping someone else.

By embracing the limits of your choice today, you can create more choices in future as you have invested your resources in a way that builds future capacity. Accept less choice today for more choice tomorrow. This tends to be the reverse of what most of us do when stressed. We take *choice* or resources from tomorrow and spend them today.

That's not to say that you shouldn't be ambitious, just be clearer and cleaner with the language you use. Most of us say "*impossible*" when we actually mean "*never been done before*" or "*I have no idea how to do that*" or "*really flipping hard.*" How can you say any of those things are impossible until you give it everything for as long as you possibly can? Impossible is only provable in the doing.

Setting out to do the extraordinarily difficult is immensely painful at times and I guarantee if you set out on that road you will have nearly everything stripped away if you are to come anywhere close to achieving your dream. So if something does inspire you that much then prepare as much as you can and do the things in this chapter.

The first thing you may want to do is to work within your current limits, invest wisely and overcome them. As this touches on one of the issues with your stress bands, I'll look at that now.

Build in Slack

One way to reduce your overall experience of stress and overwhelm is to commit to do less than you are doing. Most executives I know commit more than 100% of their available work time before they start their week. Given that there will always be surprises and unplanned issues, it's important to plan for them. You may not know what they are but you can be sure you will get them. Over the next three months aim to reach a point where you start your working week and *only 60% of your time* is committed.

Building in slack works on small things, such as allowing an extra five minutes to travel to a meeting, just as well as on the big things such as the promises you make to your board. Start with the small things such as allowing more time for your commute so you don't need to rush. If you have any free time because the surprises haven't appeared, invest it in capacity building for you or the people you care about. You will need to develop your people as you will have to delegate some important tasks to them to free up your time.

If you can't or won't increase slack (and some clients feel this way) go to option two which is to accept that your committed time is only 60% of your working week. This means you have to find time for the additional 40%. So look at your diary for the last month and calculate all your fixed commitments then budget for an additional 40% to cover all the follow up work and preparation work (to create the future) you aren't doing to allow for all these other commitments.

LTS2 and LTSN2

When you look at all your responsibilities and all the ways you spend your resources which factors fall into the LTS2 category and which fall into the LTSN2 category? These are:

Life's Too Short To...

And

Life's Too Short Not To...

I work with my clients to look at all the activities and actions they do in every area of their lives. If they are necessary and essential, then they stay. Many things are not. You may conclude that life's too short to spend it worrying about what others think or getting angry at careless or selfish car drivers. These are all things that can dramatically increase our experience of stress with no return at all.

The biggest one a client has ever placed in this category came from a senior manager in a bank. He had worked there from high school and was in his 28th year. He said, *"Life's too short to continue doing a fill-in job before I go to college."*

He had only taken a temporary job to raise money for travel before he went to university. His girlfriend became pregnant, he went full time so that they could afford to raise the child. He never managed to get to university. After 28 years, he figured it was time to find a job he enjoyed (he said that he had never liked the work he did).

What you won't see from the list of actions for "Life's Too Short to..." is anything that you are not currently doing that you really want to do. Many of us think we are clear on what is most important to us but our behaviour rarely reflects these priorities. Distractions push and pull us in different directions. So thinking about what you are not doing that you most want or even need to do can be a moving exercise. It can include things like

Life's too short Not To...

Be an active parent.

Visit my friend in hospital.

Repair my relationship with (friend/relative).

Take better care of myself.

Replenishment: Ever Fed the Ducks on a Monday?

One of my favourite business people is Ricardo Semler. He wrote a terrific book in the 1993 called *Maverick* about how he had led the transformation of his father's company. Semler had nearly killed himself playing the global executive, so he set about creating a human workplace. His follow-up book 10 years later, titled "*The Seven Day Weekend,*" is another excellent read. In it, he asks, "*Why are we able to answer emails on Sundays, but unable [to feed the ducks or] go to the movies on Monday afternoons?*"[36]

Semler makes an important point that is missed in the sincere efforts most people make to re-establish a life-work balance after a period of intense work. They may have been working 70 hours a week so they will be dramatically overdrawn in many areas of their life-physical, relational and so on. I have yet to see an organisation that encouraged its people to work 20 hours a week for a month so that they could recover fully. The best most of us manage is to get home on time that week.

If you were overdrawn at your bank and spent the next month spending only what you had earned, would your bank manager write off your overdraft? Less bad is not recovery it is merely not making things worse.

If things have been draining, shouldn't you pursue recovery as aggressively as you do sales targets or project delivery? At the very least, if you have been overextended for a long time, look for ways to recharge the batteries during work time.

Thinking about anticipation, how about letting your people have an easy week in the run up to pressurised time? I used to encourage my assistant to take time off before week long courses. I figured if she reminded her children what she looked like before going missing for a week, they would still recognise her when she reappeared. This would reduce everyone's stress levels.

The Benefits of Leaving Your People Alone

One of the biggest energy sappers for us today is interruptions. To some extent disruption and interruptions are what we are paid for. However, many are down to general overwork and pressure so everyone interrupts everyone else as they try desperately to avoid snapping. When you consider that it can take 30 minutes for someone to regain the same brain functioning that was lost to answer an "urgent" call from the boss, and that disruptions tend to spread throughout an organisation, you can start to see the importance of minimising those disruptions for everyone.[37] Most simply, this means that questions and calls are restricted to set times.

Some teams develop a triage system for all questions and requests the way an Accident and Emergency Ward conducts an immediate assessment of everyone on arrival. They nominate one team member to take all the questions for half a day and to perform a quick assessment on how critical the situation is. They either email the questions to arrive when the colleague is available or forward them immediately if they are sufficiently important. The same approach can work at the weekend too.

Some leaders are initially reluctant to store up any questions for their people. They usually become supportive when they see the benefit of reducing the interruptions they receive. Then they are usually willing to give it a try for a couple of weeks and restrict questions to every couple of hours. They can also feel able to ask that they are not interrupted at certain times so that they can do strategic work. This helps them to get ahead of events and to shape the future which can reduce the need for them to interrupt at all.

If you are serious about this you can also review what types of interruptions occur in your organisation and then work to eliminate as many as you can through better processes that anticipate peoples' needs more effectively.

Make Everything Pay for Itself

I once had a conversation with a senior project director at Richard Branson's Virgin Group. I was impressed to hear that everything at Virgin had to pay its way. For example, projects like Virgin Galactic, the space program, generate considerable PR for the company. However, the value of that PR is not in any financial calculations of project's ROI. It has to pay for itself.

Investments in any new ideas were drip fed and most resources were borrowed initially. This made any loss affordable as cost are minimised and the consequences of terminating a promising yet ultimately unprofitable idea is easy as borrowed resources are simply returned.

I encourage all my clients to make all areas of their lives sustainable from a resource perspective–at least in the medium to long term. It takes effort but it's the only way to stop sappers draining resources from everywhere else. It makes for some tough decisions as it can be hard to walk away from something you have invested years in. It's all about questioning your motives (" *Why am I doing this again?*") and your investment assumptions (" *What has to happen for this to pay off?*")

Often, you can restructure the investment so that you have a longer payback period or get more contribution from others. Other times you can find a way to invest even more to turn the problem (net resource gain) into a resource generator.

One example I see quite often in business is situations where good managers get punished for doing the right thing. For example, if you have a reputation for turning around poor performance through a commitment to people development, you can often find that you only ever get projects or teams that need turning around. You then spend all your time in the intensive recovery stage (where you have to invest most heavily). You never get the benefit of your hard work as you are moved onto the next project in crisis before the people who are now performing have repaid your investment through increased productivity.

You could restructure this situation to make it pay for everyone. You could negotiate with your manager to have an under performer's salary taken from your head count calculations. Or you could stay on the team for at least six months after they have started to perform. This allows you to recovery fully from any exertions and to help the team members become star performers. Or you could negotiate an easy assignment next time round.

If that isn't possible and other managers are not tackling under performance, then you may be better off refusing the assignment and offer to lead a six month project to improve companywide people management practices. The investment would be much bigger in the short term but you would have a chance of eliminating the worst problems completely.

'This One Doesn't Belong to Me'

Colonel Jill Chambers (US Army-Ret) is one of the finest people I know. She spent her first career in the military and her last assignment was working for General Casey and Admiral Mullen in the Pentagon to address PTSD in the US Armed Forces. This assignment began with "Does PTSD exist? Do we have a problem with it?" and culminated in the world's biggest psychology initiative, the $123m Comprehensive Soldier Fitness Program. CSF is a positive psychology program that builds mental and psychological toughness the way fitness programs build physical toughness.

Jill is now officially retired (but you wouldn't guess that from her schedule). She helps service members and their families as they transition out of the military through her charity, This Able Vet, with her equally inspiring husband, Country music star Michael Peterson.

To maximise her contribution, she has to ensure that she has the resources to maintain and build future capacity. Here's what she says about protecting boundaries and staying strong:

> "'You can't save everybody'– and when I heard that at first I thought, "But you should!" The thing is though that it isn't possible so you have to learn to say to yourself –'This challenge doesn't belong to me.'
> …There are many people I come into contact with and some are in situations that I really can't fix. I can spend a lot of energy on that to the detriment of my own

health. So sometimes it's just OK to say "And this one doesn't belong to me."

Being Willing To Walk Away

Sometimes, there is no way to make current activities pay (either today or tomorrow). If you can't restructure them, you may have to walk away. I have done this in a number of situations since my recovery. Some have been a no-cost choice so I was able to feel virtuous without having to pay for it. Other times, the right long term decision has caused severe short term strain in the business (and sometimes at home).

One individual I did a lot of work with was subtly abusive and unsupportive in many of his interactions. I realised that I couldn't sustain this relationship over the long term so I attempted to renegotiate how we worked together. I did this for nearly a year. All to no avail. So I walked.

This was terrifically expensive and having what amounted to an empty diary was extremely stressful. After that experience, I significantly increased the minimum level of trust that I needed to see and feel to work with anyone. Within a year of the empty diary, I had the busiest diary for five years and it was with partners and colleagues whose integrity and behaviour I could trust. Having persisted with this approach, I have the best group of colleagues I have ever had. Knowing they will behave with integrity and that they will consider my interests as much as they consider their own is incredibly valuable. I know they have my back and I have theirs. I have been able to create a much safer social environment.

Know What You Are Taking On

All the work we are doing here is to protect you from avoidable/unhelpful distress. More important than avoiding distress is that you are aware of and embrace the (potential) consequences of your actions. Choose with your eyes open and make sure you have the resources you need to recover so that you suffer no long-term harm. But if you are in a situation where you could suffer long term harm, be sure that you make the choice and don't be swept along by the momentum in the situation. And make sure you are doing it for the right reasons (whatever they are for you.)

To finish this set of ideas, let's have a little philosophy! The Stoic philosopher Epictetus wrote this over 2000 years ago:

"I wish to win the Olympics." But consider what comes first and what follows, and then, if it be to your advantage, set to work. You must conform to the discipline...you must give yourself to your trainer as you would to a doctor...Reflect on these things, and then, if you still wish to, go on to become a competitor.[38]

Your choices and decisions have consequences and create or add to the momentum in a situation. It is important to consider how today's decision will lead to other decisions and commitments later. To do this we need to know the difference between thinking in movies and thinking in photographs.

5b
Looking and Resources and Strengths Differently

Think in Movies and not Photographs

To understand an emerging situation, we freeze it temporarily in our minds–take a photograph if you will. We compare the situation to previous ones, form a predictive map (i.e., a picture of what we think will happen next), and then we respond.

Thought is resource intensive so you can minimise mental strain if you can work in familiar or stable situations. Then, you can quickly freeze the situation and use past experience to tackle the mismatch. You may miss out on new, creative solutions but it's efficient. In new, uncertain, or potentially threatening situations, this process can be dangerously slow as we attempt to deal with the threat by gathering more data. [This is one of the main differences between novice and expert performance.] In the time it takes to gather that data, key variables may have changed. This can create more danger and make any conclusions meaningless as everything has evolved. It's like trying to cross a road with a one minute old picture of where all the cars were.

For dynamic situations, we have to think in movies, not in photographs. We still need to freeze the picture. It's just that we need to do it quickly and then keep taking pictures as we figure out what to do. We then compare each frame so that we appreciate the **direction** and the **speed** of the situation.

This may sound challenging (and it is), but you do it all the time with familiar situations–crossing a busy street, for example. There you consider all the different variables moving at different speeds and directions and imagine yourself crossing (factoring in your current fitness and ability to move) until you find a safe answer.

To do this in new, more complex situations, you need a deeper understanding of the critical variables and crucially how those elements relate to and affect each other. This comes through mastery. Mastery allows you to "*take a situation whole*" to paraphrase the *Sun Tzu*. You will also be able to act skilfully without conscious thought. This is why preparation and experience are so helpful in reducing stress.

Lessons from Triathlon–It's all about the Transition and the Next Activity

As part of my recovery I took up triathlon (swim, cycle and run). I was surprised to find that the biggest benefit from being a triathlete was not improved fitness but in how it has changed my approach to work. To succeed at triathlon, you must connect each discipline. You need to swim in a way that has the smallest impact on your ability to cycle; and cycle in a way that maximises your potential run speed. This means you need to generate most propulsion from your arms when swimming to save your legs for cycling. And you adjust your riding position on the bike so that it is closer to running. These adjustments make you slightly slower in the swim and cycle, but faster overall.

There's a fourth discipline too–transitions. That's the time when you run out of the water and change into your cycling gear and later when you jump off your bike to get ready for the run. It's important to get this right as it can save you two minutes or more in a race.

The lesson from these seemingly separate activities is to link them together in ways that help you to quickly regain your balance, recover, and be ready for the next challenge. By focusing less on each individual task or activity and more on their relationship between each other, you can minimise the negative impact and maximise the positive momentum one activity can create for the next, and the next and the next...

Get off the Beach

A helpful military analogy of focusing through a task and transition to the next task comes from retired USMC Colonel Mike Wyly. Mike used to teach amphibious warfare in the US Marine Corps. One of the most important lessons was to ensure the Marines had the aim of getting off the beach and not simply to land on the beach.

The landing is such an important part of the mission that it is easy to get fixated on that and forget it is only the beginning. The landing needs to be completed in a way that makes getting off the beach as quick and as safe as possible.[39]

Sometimes I actually repeat "*Get off the beach*" to myself as I tackle a stressor. It reminds me of the real goal: tackle what's in front in such a way that I can recover and be ready for the next challenge.

Your performance right now as you read this may be affected by what you have just been doing (or even what you have been doing a few days ago). And that transitioning between different activities is crucial to maximise your productivity. It's all connected. If you accept that one thing leads to another you can begin to link things together consciously. This can lead to surprisingly large productivity gains and energy savings as you realise that in some situations going faster now will only get you to the next road block a little quicker. Far better to drive at a speed that allows you to minimise road blocks and hold up. For that, you need to adapt your thinking.

Think in Movies in Your Work and Life

When going through your day/week/month, it's helpful to think of what you've spent, what you have available and what your future commitments/ deposits are going to be. Plan for where you want to be. Take it easy before an important event so you are totally prepared. Stop taking calls 5-10 minutes before an important meeting so that you get into the optimal emotional state.

It's also important to consider the longer trend. Ask, "Where is my current narrative heading? If things stay as they are, where am I going to end up in 1, 2, 30 years' time?" It was asking these types of questions, and allowing myself to accept the future I had created (through my daily actions) that I realized I couldn't get out of my trouble on my own.

Russ Ackoff, one of the top business thinkers of the 20th Century, said that your future is already here in the present "*mess*" you are living in.[40] Let's look at the mess I was in. I had suffered from depression on and off all my life and had refused to take any medication. I had made it through each episode myself. [Most of us suffer low moods; it's really the same as suffering the flu.]

Early in 2009, I had been suffering the most severe depression of my life for nearly 18 months. This was the worst it had ever been but I was still refusing to take medication. I was also 245lb, approximately 70lb (five stone) overweight. I had no work in the diary and was making no real progress in finding it. I also had debts that would make some countries blush. Where was this story going? Where was the momentum? If it was a film what would you expect to happen to this character? I could see only negative outcomes. There was no happy ending, no champagne lounge. The momentum was all the wrong way. The solution had now gone beyond me. So I went to see the doctor and finally took the pills.

I was feeling noticeably stronger within a month. I was no bundle of light but I found that I had enough momentum to start making calls in a more constructive way. A month or two after that I was invited to tender for a piece of work that led to a three year engagement. I also began moving more physically and started to change the future health mess by clearing up the present one.

I only took the pills for six weeks so there long term involvement in this story was low. What I think may have made as much difference as the chemical shift was my acceptance of where I was. My friend, organizational transformation specialist, Andy Pellant, says that the single biggest cause of company failures is a lack of agreement and acceptance between the senior leaders of where a company is and where it is heading.

So find a way to accept where your story is heading. If you don't like the direction, change today's actions to change the longer term narrative.

Don't Mortgage the Future for Today

If stressors are temporary and instructive and we have time for recovery we can invest in future building. So ask yourself: *"After this, what then?"* If this is a one-off shock and everything else is stable, spend away. If it's a great opportunity, you can even take resources from tomorrow and spend them on today's challenge as long as it increases tomorrow's capacity.

If that stressor is more persistent (chronically stressful) or if you are simply going to move from this stressor to another, you need to focus on your recovery and how you will recoup your spending. Dynamic environments punish borrowing if you don't use it to build capacity. If what you are doing today doesn't increase capacity tomorrow, the mismatch between demands and capacity and desire will widen. You will have to come through today's challenge, by dropping into a potentially vicious progress trap.

A progress trap happens when you "solve" a problem today in a way that only creates an even bigger problem tomorrow. An example of this would be an athlete taking steroids. The seemingly small decision to boost performance with drugs leads to lots of other problems. Steroids and other short term boosts usually lead to vicious progress traps and much bigger problems in the future. [Ask Lance Armstrong about this one if you wonder if this is true.]

Sometimes the only answer to impossible short term demands is goal sacrificing. At other times there are things you can do. One of the most useful is to tackle your boiled frogs and muffins before you need to.

Embrace Boiled Frogs and Muffins!

You may have heard of the story of the boiled frog. As a quick reminder, if you throw a frog into boiling water, so the story goes, it will jump out immediately and be largely unharmed. Place the same frog in a pan of cool water and gently raise the heat, the frog will eventually roll onto its back and be cooked alive. The changes to the frog's environment were so incrementally small it didn't notice it was in trouble and so it died when it could have saved itself.

I have never actually tested the frog theory so I hesitate to rely on it. However, one theory I have tested to failure is the *"One Muffin at a Time"* theory. And I think a combination of Boiled Frog and One Muffin may explain much of the trouble people face with stress.

I accept I'm doing some serious metaphor mixing here—*"The Frog who ate too many muffins and boiled himself"* principle is unlikely to catch on at Harvard Business School, but stay with me as there is something in both stories.

At my heaviest, I weighed 17 ½ stone (245lb) (or 111kg in Euros. I am 5'8" so *"unhealthy"* is an understatement. Now that I have lost that weight and am in the best shape of my life, some people are courageous or rude enough to ask me:

"How did you get that big?!"

Most expect some dramatic stories of all–you–can–eat buffets. The answer is as simple as it is banal, *"One muffin at a time."* I didn't wake up one day and gorge myself. It took me over five years of surprisingly easy, consistent effort to gain the five stones. Five stone in five years–that's 14lbs a year–just over 1lb a month. This means I needed just one unnecessary, supersized muffin a week (and to ignore the feedback). That's all. Nothing dramatic. Just one simple, easily missed habit.

Who knew, right? So the question isn't how I did it, but why more people don't because it is so easy to get off track if you stop looking ahead to see where the route is taking you, or where the movie is headed. In my case, it was straight to the concession stand for another muffin!

Crashes Never Happen Quickly

People who crash are rarely more than a few degrees out. The crash happens at such speed we assume that they must have been doing something dreadfully wrong. Not so. A disaster happens one muffin at a time and one degree of heat at a time.

Every crash I have seen (and been a part of) had two main causal factors. Firstly, the person had some unhelpful habits that were gradually eroding capacity and desire (which was ignored) to a crucial tipping point. The speed comes from the second factor: a change in the environment (ticking over from 99 to 100 degrees). The change is dramatic but the build-up isn't. Stretch to snap in one final step.

Ignore the signs and one day you wake up and realise you are one heavy frog in really hot water! So this could easily happen to any of us if our environment became more challenging. To minimise the chance of this, we need to make our muffins and their compounding consequences more visible and sort them out.

Secret Muffin Eaters of the World...

If you look around, you can see a lot of people eating an extra muffin a week either literally or metaphorically. Most executives are broadly successful with a few muffins. That is, they have a few unhelpful, resource draining habits that never get called out.

Maybe a leader is a little too controlling. There are balancing weights that keep them safe and the environment they are in doesn't call them out. Sometimes their people complain (to each other) but it never gets out of hand until things move so fast. Then a crisis hits and everyone sits around waiting to see what the boss will do now. The delay and lack of trust turns a crisis into a potential disaster.

What Are Your Muffins?

What muffins do you have? That is, habits which aren't helping but don't appear to be causing you any real problems—yet. Take a good look at what you are doing and look to develop healthier habits that can help increase your capacity. If the action doesn't help you create a successful narrative, cut it out of the story completely. It took me years to gain all that weight but I started having tighter clothes within the first year. But I was so busy; I did nothing about it and gave it a nice sounding description (I was becoming cuddly!) Messed up thinking.

The muffin principle will help you to reduce your drain on resources. What else can you do to ensure you have the resources for today's work and still have enough to invest in tomorrow's capacity and desire?

Longer Term Resource and Strength Work

In this chapter so far, we have been looking at your resource spend and how to reduce it. By using stress bands and movie thinking you can better understand the implications of your current actions on the future. This makes it easier for you to change what you are doing now to create a more harmonious future with a smaller mismatch between demands and your capacity/desire. In the final section, we are going to look at a different way in which you can view your resources and resourcefulness.

To win, John Boyd said you should, *"probe and test an adversary and their allies* **to unmask strengths, weaknesses, maneuvers, and intentions**."[41] Once done, you could begin to understand how you could win. Few of us have an actual opponent, so we can take this as encouragement for us to probe and test the external environment. This gives us an insight in the challenges you need to overcome if you are to win. Also, it is crucial that we understand and clarify your own *"strengths, weaknesses, maneuvers and intentions."* This insight will give us the best way to be more creative and *resourceful* with our resources.

You need to understand the resources you have available, how fast you can respond to a challenge, and what it is likely to cost you. You may have noted in the quote that Boyd says "<u>probe and test</u>" and not just measure. The only way to see what you are capable of is to find a way to test it. It is also important to learn which situations or challenges give you the best chance to use your strengths. Spending more and more time in situations or environments that suit you make it easiest to create a match between the external demands and your capacity and desires.

Being challenged in an area where you have high levels of mastery is likely to be challenging but enjoyable because you have surplus capacity. Also, demonstrating mastery tends to stimulate positive emotions (which keep resources topped up). This can increase desire so even a tough week at the office is likely to be developmental.

However, being tested in an area where you have little skill, experience and/or resources is likely to generate negative stress. Having to behave in an unskilled way can also reduce our desire as it's harder to feel we are making progress when our performance is relatively poor compared to times when we can operate at our best in known situations.

Actions and Intentions–What is Success?

Success Built to Last is an exceptional book written by three authors, Porras, Emery, and Thompson.[42] The book studies people the authors call *builders* (named after the concept of clock-builders popularised by Porras and his co-author, Jim Collins in the business classic *Built to Last.*) A clock-builder is not someone who can only tell the time (or achieve something) today, but someone who builds a clock that creates that ability for them or their organisation to achieve the goal for years or decades. Consequently, the criteria for inclusion into the study was that a leader had enjoyed at least 20 years of success.

At the start of the book, they refer to a conversation with Peter Drucker who told them that most studies on the behaviours of successful leaders failed because:

"Until you 'figure out what success means' to you personally and to your organisation, leadership is an almost 'pointless conversation,' Drucker admonished."

When you consider your actions and goals or intentions to what extent are they based on your definition of success? What is success to you? The authors go on to say that all the builders they interviewed saw success as:

"a life and work that brings personal fulfilment and lasting relationships and makes a difference in the world in which they live."

Even though this may be out of the scope of our 90 day focus I encourage you to begin engaging with the question, *"What is success to me?"*

Gallup's Distinctions for Strengths and Weaknesses

It's helpful for us to be clearer on what strengths are and are not. The most useful distinctions I have seen for strengths and weaknesses come from the Gallup organisation.[43] They make a distinction between talents, strengths, non-talents and weaknesses.

Talents–*"Recurring pattern of thought, feeling or behaviour that can be productively applied."*

Strengths–*"Consistent, near perfect performance in an activity."*

Non-Talents–*Actions or activities for which you have demonstrated little or no aptitude.*

Weaknesses–*A non-talent you must now rely on to do your job successfully.*

When environments change, new demands can make non–talents essential. As soon as they are required to do your job, the non–talent turns into a weakness. Given that they are actions or activities for which you have shown little or no aptitude, this can have an enormous, negative impact on performance.. It's vital then that you are clear about your TSNWs. This will give you a much clearer picture of the resources you have and what you can do with them.

The World's Greatest Organisational Motto

The motto of the US Marine Corp is *Semper Fidelis – Always faithful.* Unlike most corporate mottos "Semper Fi" means a great deal to the Marines I know.[44]

I have created an acronym based on the USMC motto. This relates to the key resources and strengths needed to achieve your goals. The acronym stands for:

Spiritual
Emotional
Mental
Physical
External (Resources)
Relational
Fidelis

A helpful approach is to imagine each type of resource held in a tank or store. As you go through the day, week, or year, these stores are used up and/or replenished. The degree to which you have a strength in that area will influence the return you are able to generate from using the resource. A combination of all six areas will help you to remain strong and resilient as you shape your future. I will take these in turn.

Spiritual/Emotional Resources and Strengths

Spiritual and emotional resources and strengths may not seem to be that important for you in dealing with stressful situations. They are probably the most important. As we have discussed many times already, your emotional strength and control are crucial if you are to behave in the most constructive way.

I am not referring to a belief in god when I refer to spiritual (but it has been shown to help if you do believe). In this context it refers to a belief that your work matters more than just for the work itself. It is also affected by your connection to a coherent and inspiring past. The stronger the connection to a noteworthy history, the stronger you are going to be. If you perceive no connection between your actions today and those of your past you are going to be more challenged in difficult times as you have less to fall back on.

The USMC are masters at helping their Marines to see the rich traditions, of which each one is a part. The US Military Academy at West Point is the same. A West Point Graduate is part of the Long Gray Line of leaders who have passed through officer training. It's something to live up to.

Boyd spoke about cultivating moral (spiritual and emotional in my model), mental and physical strength. I have included some of his comments in this section on these strengths in italics. [45] Here is what he said about moral strength:

Avoid mismatches between what we say we are, what we are, and the world we have to deal with, as well as by abiding by those other cultural codes or standards that we are expected to uphold.

This is an excellent definition of "*integrity.*" The root of integrity is the same as "*integer*"–meaning "*one*" or "*whole.*" Integrity helps you to match all parts of your life. As situations demand faster and faster responses, having people with integrity becomes even more significant as the speed of the situation will mean they have to make decisions on their own. During those times, you really need them to behave with integrity. Here is what Warren Buffet said about integrity in a 1998 to a group of MBA students[46]:

> "*In fact, there was a fellow, Pete Kiewit in Omaha, who used to say, he looked for three things in hiring people: integrity, intelligence and energy. And he said if the person did not have the first two, the latter two would kill him. Because if they don't have integrity, you want them dumb and lazy–you don't want them smart and energetic!*"

A lack of integrity can seem to be increasingly prevalent In spite of the many transgressions of integrity we see in the press, such as politicians abusing expenses or athletes taking PEDs. However, I think there is an increasingly powerful momentum towards integrity. This is because it is becoming increasingly difficult to show a lack of integrity and get away with it. That is why so many people get caught out.

In addition, as the boundaries between different areas of our lives blur, it's increasingly difficult to act differently between work and home, for example. At some point, the domains will come together and then you will have an enormous, self-inflicted mismatch to resolve. If the difference is stylistic then the mismatch will be relatively easy to rectify. If the difference is moral, then you will have a great deal of trouble.

Mismatches between you and your environment in this domain are usually the hardest to reconcile and the most stressful. These mismatches create stress as nearly every interaction becomes a mismatch of core philosophy or modus operandi.

When considering your Spiritual and Emotional resources and strengths, ask questions like these: What are your values and what do you value? What is most important to you? How do you resolve challenges to what matters most to you? If someone was observing you, what would they suggest mattered most from what they saw? In your key environments, organizational and in your home community, what cultural values and standards are most prevalent? To what extent do these reflect your values and your preferred culture? Looking at all the different cultures in which you have lived, which has been the closest match to how you prefer to work? What qualities or values are most important for you to have met in this area for you to perform at your best?

Mental Resources and Strengths

This also includes your thought processes and how you think about what happens around you. What do you do to understand your environment? What could you do to improve your mental processes? Do you have clear processes or check lists to simplify the task as much as you can to improve your thinking in turbulent situations? This will give you the best chance to be at your best when it matters.

When considering mental resources, Boyd said:

> *[Select] information from a variety of sources or channels in order to generate mental images or impressions that match-up with the world of events or*

happenings that we are trying to understand and cope with.

Questions to think about here include: Where do you gather your information? What independent sources do you have? What can you do to improve the quality of your information sources – your intelligence to use a military phrase? How do you combine hard and soft sources of intelligence? What sources do you use and rely on to figure out what is going on and what to do when you don't know what to do? How often do you listen to the "old hands"–the people who have seen a number of organizational transitions? What do you do to handle ambiguity? What would it take for you to be more comfortable suspending your conclusions and still be actively engaged in what is happening?

Physical Resources and Strengths

The most obvious resource here is your physical endurance. Physical endurance can make an enormous difference in determining if you are able to thrive or even just survive turbulent times. But what did Boyd say about physical resources?

[Open] up and maintain many channels of communication with the outside world, hence with others out there, that we depend upon for sustenance, nourishment, or support.

He emphasises your connection with the outside world. I would extend this to include any place where you get physical sustenance, nourishment, or support. We will cover in Chapter 8 how to accelerate your physical recovery and find relatively easy ways to strengthen your physical reserves so that you have more in the tank, so to speak, when you are put under pressure.

Sustained stress can prompt us to do things that reduce our physical resilience in the short and long term. For example, to hit a deadline, we often skip physical exercise for a week or two. Stopping something temporarily is fine. However, this can go one for weeks and then months and we never restart our program as things don't calm down. What you must do is to <u>put a note in your diary to restart the sustaining activity you have stopped.</u> That way you ensure it is only temporary.

Thinking of your physical space, to what extent is it a restful and safe environment? How relaxing and nourishing do you find it? What could you do to improve that?

External Resources and Strengths

This links to what Boyd meant about physical connections. I define these as anything external to our being that we can potentially use to help us achieve our goals. When we get into a stressful situation the time pressure becomes so great that we either forget to ask for help or we conclude that it would be quicker to do everything ourselves. Fine if the situation quickly ends but dangerous if the challenge lasts a long time. When we voluntarily reduce our own access to external resources, we make an assumption about how long the additional load will last. So, as I encourage with a decision to stop exercise for a few weeks, make your assumptions explicit. For example,

> *"I am choosing to do this extra work myself because I think being short staffed will last only two weeks and it isn't worth training someone to do it. I think I could do this for four weeks before it starts to create a strain in other areas. Therefore, I will review my two week assumption on x date."*

Other forms of resources and support include such things as administrative support; getting absolutely clear on what you need to do vs. what you can give to others and acting accordingly; development of a more supportive culture in your team; investing in long term friendships; creating a group of helpers such as fitness coaches, therapists, business coaches etc. who could help you stay out of trouble (or recover from trouble). Even if you don't use them, it's helpful to know where to go in advance if you did.

Having workplace mentors (both inside and outside your company) is an excellent way to increase your ability to see the bigger picture. This can help you to get ahead of the situation and leave you better prepared for the future. All these things can be immensely helpful in creating a safe social environment.

It is also worth looking at the resources that can or could help you in all areas of your life. One very highly rated partner in a professional service firm I worked with had an equally successful wife. To give them a chance of any free time at the weekend, they employed a university student to do their chores (shopping, dry cleaning etc.) and even got her a credit card to pay for things. This saved them time that they were able to spend on renewal activities with their children.

Relational Resources and Strengths

Linked to external are the relations you have with those around you. Strong, positive relations with others as you go through challenging situations are more valuable than gold. What do you do to nurture strong, mutually supportive relationships with people in all areas of your life? Hardly anyone would ever suggest that friends and able and loyal colleagues were not valuable, but does your behaviour reflect this? Do you really invest in them? When you think of the relationships that are most important to you, to what extent does your time and energy investments reflect that?

In the Care and Support section, we will be speaking about "*4am friends*"– people who you could call at 4am if you were in trouble and be sure they'd come to your aid. Do you have one or even are you lucky enough to have two? Thinking about the people on whom you rely to achieve what you do (and not just in work), what is the quality of those relationships? How do you measure effective relationships? What could you do to strengthen them?

Fidelis

Fidelis refers to the level of consistency you bring to all six key resources. A sports coach once said "*Consistency precedes excellence.*" What levels of resources and resourcefulness can you bring to every situation? If you are ever short of resources, what can you do to ensure your resourcefulness makes up for the lack of resources? How aware are you of the quantity and quality of your resources in this area? Do you have a problem with your consistency? If so, you will be able to improve it dramatically with the exercises and ideas in this book.

Questions

-    What are the trends, patterns, and directions of your day? For example, are there immediate pressures early on or does pressure build slowly? How about trends and patterns in your week or month? What events seem to happen fairly frequently? What kinds of surprises do you get? Are there predictable surprises? [I know this sounds silly but you will be amazed at the patterns to surprises that can emerge when you pay attention to things you hadn't planned for. Surprises reveal mismatches and gaps in our understanding so they are worth our time.]

- What do you do to ensure you have the energy you need for your most important tasks? What is the best build up for a big meeting or important piece of work?

- What is your preferred rhythm or tempo? Do you prefer to start slow and build or sprint with periods of rest? How could you structure your time to more closely match this preference?

- What can you do to create more coherence among all the different things that you do? Are there themes that you could draw together? What are the individual situations all about? If there are no coherent themes, what can you do to improve that?

- Is it possible for you to structure parts of your week or month for specific activities such as admin, strategy, financial work, etc.? Remember the goal here is to build and then maintain momentum for the best results. The fewer changes you have to make the faster you can go.

- What could you do to reduce the impact of distractions and interruptions? Can you contract with your colleagues and stakeholders to give you decent blocks of time for you to concentrate fully on specific tasks with interruptions limited only to absolute emergencies?

- Feed all these disruptions into your map of reality (you didn't predict it so there is something you don't understand), and start to anticipate them and eliminate them from your day.

Summary

- It's crucial to know your resource/energy spend as well as a diligent person knows where their money is going.

- Most of us are chronically over-extended and compromise family and future capacity building to pay for today. As the challenge is only going to get tougher, it's crucial you get through today with capacity and resources for the most important things including future capacity building.

- Most of us spend our energy without thinking about replenishing it. Before committing to anything, be sure to ask "Can I afford this?" and "How will I recover the energy?" Think in Movies, not photographs.

- When doing anything, be sure you aim to "*Get off the Beach*" as the Marines do. Return to your recovery point so that you can be ready to go again.

- You can use Stress Bands to help understand where your current narrative is heading. Avoid snap, choose your stretch, build capacity and reduce fixed costs.

- Contrary to popular delusion, you can't have it all and impossible is impossible. So choose what you are going to aim for.

- Mastery of anything allows intense resource conservation. Find time to reduce commitments you have made, focusing on the ones that will help you win today and tomorrow and build inspiring levels of mastery in your chosen field.

From now on we will be focusing primarily on the second ABCs. Some of the tools are still useful to help you anticipate and accelerate to meet a challenge, apply the brakes more skilfully and reduce the cost of the stress you experience. I am now going to give you more theory on the stress response and offer you other tools and techniques that will help you to deliver expert levels of performance in more and more challenging situations.

6.
Understanding the Stress Response

We are now going to look at the physiology and psychology of stress. This will deepen the work you have already done on your stress curves both for anticipation and recovery.[47] It should give you a clearer explanation of why I have made the recommendations in the book so far. This understanding will help you to make even better choices about how you deal with stressors in your life.

Before we go any further, let's revisit our definition of how stress is caused.

Stress occurs when there is a mismatch between the demands of our environment and our immediate ability and desire to adapt and recover.

What Happens When We Experience a Mismatch?

A mismatch activates the Autonomic Nervous System [autonomic simply means automatic as it operates without conscious thought]. The best known part of this system for stress is the *fight/flight* response.[48] This is controlled by a branch of the ANS, called the Sympathetic Nervous System (SNS). The SNS prepares your body for a physical challenge or some form of combat (fight/flight). In the modern world where stressors are hardly ever physical this response is often unhelpful. Before I get into more about the response I want to say a little about how the brain determines the appropriate response to a challenge (and why the response is nearly always a maladaptation).

What Happens in Your Brain?

In the 1950s and 1960s, a US physician called Paul Maclean, transformed our view of how the brain operates. Maclean argued that there are essentially three layers to the brain. Whilst they are not actually separate, they do have specific functions, and in one paper, Maclean related these layers to the evolution of animals. There are more detailed views of the brain today, but we are going to focus on Maclean's work because, rather like Newton being sufficient for daily use instead of Einstein, Maclean is as much as we need for our work on stress.

The oldest part of the brain at the top of the spine is the *R-complex* (Reptilian-complex), and it controls instinctive responses essential to daily life. This area is out of our direct control and largely follows precedence.

Jumping to the top or outer area, we have the neo–cortex. This is where our advanced thinking occurs. To continue Maclean's animal analogy, it is called the mammalian brain. If we perceive a stressful situation as safe (or even exciting), we are unlikely to do anything that is strange or unhelpful. This is because the sense of safety will keep our neo–cortex available and we will be able to think fairly clearly.

Unfortunately for work situations (but fortunately for life and death situations) to get to the neo–cortex, you have to get through the middle layer of the brain, which constitutes *the limbic system*. The limbic brain controls our emotional life. Emotions are crucial as they tell us to like things we determine are good for us and to dislike things that are not. For example, feeling sick if we smell bad food, loving our children, disliking people who have harmed us all change the energy (and motivation) we have available to us.

The limbic system then ensures we have the energy to execute that decision. This energy generating part may be the most important role of emotions. What's particularly useful is that we don't have to waste too much time "*thinking*" about these things. This ability to move at speed is crucial in stressful situations.

Figure 7: MacLean's Triune Brain

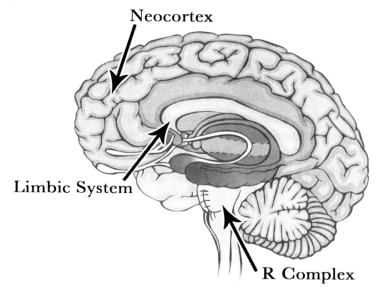

As the limbic brain is absolutely pivotal to the stress response, we'll look at that more closely now.

How you Assess a Stressor

A key part of the limbic brain is the amygdala. It monitors all raw data coming into the brain, and it acts as an early warning system. Scientists used to think that the more advanced part of the brain, the neo–cortex, did this. And when things are calm, it does seem to handle most of the work. However, the amygdala is always on and takes control in challenging, or potentially threatening situations. If the situation is deemed to be sufficiently threatening, the limbic brain can actually shut down the neo–cortex completely.

The amygdala is constantly looking for potential threats, effectively asking two questions–"*Is this new or not new? Is it a threat or not a threat?*" To answer these questions, it communicates with another part of the limbic brain–the hippocampus, which links memory storage and retrieval. Based on previous experience/ information, the amygdala sends a signal to a third key part of the limbic brain, the hypothalamus. On receipt of the assessment, the hypothalamus then instructs the body to release the hormones needed to respond to the threat as it has been interpreted.

When assessing a threat, your brain has the past and the immediate moment as potential sources of information. The future is irrelevant if your life is at stake. The greater the perceived threat, the less memory you will be able to access. This is because stress hormones flood the brain and impede connections in the neo–cortex. The higher levels of the brain get shut down the brain needs lots of blood to be fully operation and in a life and death situation, that blood many be needed in the body.

The Limbic Brain–Fast, but Vague

The amygdala makes assessments faster than the neo–cortex. But it achieves this speed at the cost of being vague. The neo–cortex is slower and more precise. For example, if you were walking through a garden and saw what looked like a snake, your amygdala would prompt you to instinctively jump back. Your more discerning

123

cortex would send a message a little later, "*Don't worry it's just a hose pipe.*"

Having your emotional brain responding without thought has saved us through our evolution. But, it also is why you can find yourself saying or doing things you later regretted as you reacted to a perceived threat before considering the most helpful long-term response.

To keep our thinking clear in turbulent situations we have to find better ways of working with the limbic brain. Relying on primitive limbic responses doesn't help us in most work place situations. It is almost impossible to improve this relationship the moment a threat is perceived. We can do it in advance though by considering our potential answers to the "*new/not new?*" and "*threat/no threat?*" questions. This anticipatory work effectively creates "future memories" our hippocampus can access when it is asked to compare the new experience with our memories of previous situations.

If you are able to practice enough, your response becomes habitual and no longer requires conscious thought. You will be able to perform under pressure. This gives us a chance to keep our emotional brain at helpful levels of activation and dramatically reduce the stress chemicals our body produces.

So what are these stress chemicals? Where do they come from? What do they do?

Being Fed Energy We Hardly Ever Need

The hormones produced by the body in response to a stressor are key element in a wonderfully fast, yet complex, process that prepares you for battle. Your focus is sharpened and narrows on the perceived threat; energy increases in the body; your pulse and blood pressure increase as blood is moved from non-essential areas such as the brain to the limbs. This primes us for the fight/flight response.

The first hormones that increase energy and prepare the body for fight/flight are noradrenalin and adrenalin. (As they perform broadly the same function, I'll be referring to them both as adrenalin). This hormone takes around 10 to 15 seconds to respond. If the challenge persists for a few minutes then another hormone, cortisol, is pushed into the blood stream. Adrenalin is faster acting than cortisol—it's the hormonal equivalent of chocolate. Cortisol is slower but much longer lasting – more like a starchy carbohydrate as it can take more than 12 hours to leave your system after a strong, negative stress response. Adrenaline is crucial for the phasic activation I mentioned earlier and cortisol is the key hormone for tonic activation.

Our bodies are feeding us a diet of hormones, most importantly, cortisol, which supply enough energy to run a marathon or to fight a bear. As our stress is hardly ever physical, this is like eating piles of pasta and chocolate sitting at our desks. This is the physiological source of most of our troubles with stress in our environment today.

Cortisol, so crucial for the longer periods of activation, is seen as the bogeyman of the stress response. In fact, it is a misunderstood and misused source of energy.

Cortisol - The "Stress Hormone"

If your body is functioning well, cortisol levels peak when you wake up. And that is actually why you wake up. You have been raised to consciousness by a spiking of cortisol levels. Cortisol slowly declines throughout the day as it is used up. Then you fall back to sleep. During sleep, your body produces more and wakes you up in the morning to start all over again.

Cortisol is known as the "stress hormone" because high stress leads to excessive cortisol levels. Chronic stress can leave you with persistently elevated cortisol levels which can lead to the short term illnesses I mentioned in the introduction. And this elevated cortisol is a key reason why you can't relax and may find it hard to sleep when you are going through turbulence.

Ironically, this overload takes such a toll that it also makes it impossible for your body to produce the cortisol early in the morning so you find yourself needing more and more external stimulants such as sugary foods or coffee to get up in the morning.

The Body's Brakes–Our Recovery System and Alternative Energy Source

Recall the surge of energy you experienced the last time you had to respond quickly to a physical threat—such as almost getting run over. The initial surge of energy that helped you jump to safety didn't actually come from adrenalin and cortisol, the accelerators we've just been talking about. The energy boost actually came from your body releasing the brakes. Your "brakes" in this context are the activities of the parasympathetic nervous system (PNS).

The PNS handles things like digestion, cellular repair/renewal, and sexual reproduction. Immediately stopping renewal activity and making that energy available for the emergency makes up for the 10 to 15 seconds the adrenalin takes to work. The PNS also brings the body back to normal levels once a threat is over (it applies the brakes). It does this by sending a neurotransmitter called acetylcholine to "tell" the activated systems—heart, blood flow, etc., to stand down and return to normal. [A neurotransmitter is just a chemical that the body uses to facilitate communication through the nerves of your body.]

The PNS clearly does more than simply handle the brakes. You can see it as a car management system that monitors and maintains all the (body's) key functions and maintains and improves them if it gets a chance. The closest thing in car terms would be the management and braking system of a hybrid car, such as the Toyota Prius.

The system on the Prius monitors and maintains all the car's systems and converts some energy to electricity that it stores energy in batteries to use later. If energy needs are moderate, this stored energy can meet your needs and the more powerful petrol system remains relatively inactive. This is what we want for the PNS and SNS - have a PNS which is strong enough to meet normal energy needs so that we don't need to activate the SNS.

The Benefits of a Better Braking System

If your PNS is strong enough, that is, if there's enough stored energy in the batteries to meet the needs of the environment, you can dramatically curtail the SNS led fight-flight response as your body won't need the extra energy it provides. You may still get some adrenalin that you don't need, but a swift walk will use that up.

The most important goal is to find ways to reduce unnecessary cortisol production. We can minimise this if we can prompt the recovery response within two minutes – the approximate time it takes for cortisol production to get going. You can accelerate quickly, respond well, and then return to a normal resting state.

An Ancient Circuit with Troublesome Side Effects

The psychiatrist, Professor Stephen Porges (whom I mentioned earlier) is the world's leading authority on how the ANS connects with, and is affected by, the external (social) environment. He has developed something called the Polyvagal Theory.

The "*vagal*" in his theory is the vagus nerve, which handles the most important communication between the brain, the heart and the rest of the body. Porges has uncovered some interesting (and ancient) circuitry. Professor Porges discovered that "*fight/flight*" is not a two part system but a much more intricate three part system. It's really "*fight/flight/freeze.*"

According to Porges, the freeze response prompts a huge drop in oxygen consumption, blood pressure, heart rate and any other form of physiological activation. This mimics reptiles that "*play dead*" when faced with a much larger enemy. In spite of the imminent threat.

This is rarely a useful strategy for humans as it leaves you at the mercy of your environment/stressor. Some people who have experienced severe trauma can lose the ability to move. They dissociate or disconnect from what is happening and may even lose all consciousness. The situation has become so threatening the system shuts down.

Exactly why we do this is uncertain. It could be our body's last attempt to keep us alive. It perceives that neither fight-flight will be of use so it resorts to freezing. This could protect the viability of the system in the hope that the resources saved by avoiding fighting will mean there are resources for recovery. Also, it offers our opponent the clearest possible sign of total victory and that we pose no further threat. This could persuade them to stop attacking. It could also be because we have some ancient wiring from evolution that serves little or no constructive purpose today, a neurological appendix, if you will.

Even if we can't state definitively why the freeze response exists, we can recognise that this can be enormously damaging in the wrong situations. The good news is that if we can strengthen our PNS and increase mastery then we can minimise the chance of this happening.

Building a Better Braking System is Hard

For the PNS to begin recovery after a stress response, it needs to know the danger has passed. However, if you have excessively high cortisol, the PNS will be delayed in restarting. This is because your hormone levels are saying you are still in danger. Recovery will have to wait.

At work, it can take a major shift in our environment for our stress levels to fall enough to give our bodies the all clear. For example, some executives only get the safe signal when they go on holiday. We know this because they fall ill the moment they leave the office!

If this has happened to you, it's because the SNS used all available resources to keep you going through a crisis. Some of these resources should have been spent on recovery and renewal. If we ever found ourselves in a fight with a predator, our bodies are able to even suppress feelings of pain. This is the same response over a much longer time frame. Once the danger has finally passed, (your holiday is a big safety signal), your body collapses and sets about clearing up the mess the stress response has created. So we need to find ways to turn off the fight/flight response in the SNS and to signal to the PNS that it's safe to begin renewal and recovery work.

Another challenge to strengthening your PNS is that it goes against the conventional response all my clients have adopted when faced with a stressful situation. In order to find the capacity to complete the tough challenge they neglected the things that would maintain and strengthen their PNS-things like a healthy diet, plenty of restful sleep, regular exercise, a positive emotional state. The attitude we need to cultivate is not:

"I'm so busy today, I don't have time to exercise...eat healthily...sleep."

But:

"I'm so busy today, I must be sure to exercise...eat the most nutritious foods...sleep peacefully."

It sounds crazy but once you have mastered most of the short term crises you can begin to think this way. You will see that the logic is ultimately irrefutable for lives that are chronically stressful.

If we are simply going to get another equally deserving acute stressor tomorrow, a.k.a. a crisis, then it makes no sense to treat today's crisis as life and death and compromise our future for it. Today is just another day in paradise. If we can respond to the situation without generating a fight/flight driven emotion we won't get carried away by the momentum in the situation and we can dramatically reduce our physiological response.

I will be devoting one of the longest chapters of the book to ways to strengthen the PNS. Before we do that, I would like to bring stress and emotions more closely together. Given the amount we have covered so far in this chapter, I will summarise the key points here before linking the body's response to stress to our emotions.

Summary

- The stress response is perfect for handling infrequent, acute physical challenges. This creates problems when your challenges are incessant, chronic, and mostly mental or emotional.
- To bridge this gap, we need to help our brain to assess threats more accurately. This is relatively straightforward if we do it in advance. In anticipating future challenges we need to ask "What's new/familiar about this?" And "What could I do to make this safe?"
- Cortisol is seen as the bogeyman of the stress response but it is simply an essential energy source that we overproduce.
- If we can limit the size of the stress response (and how much cortisol our bodies produce) we can have more phasic responses and avoid longer tonic responses.

- One of the best ways to do this is to improve our PNS, which can supply moderate energy needs and also activate our recovery response. This gives us more control over the power in stressful situations.

6a.
Bringing Stress and Emotions Together

Anyone working to achieve higher levels of performance with lower activation needs to cultivate more appropriate or helpful emotional states for that particular situation. The first thing I often remind my clients who may resist this suggestion that emotions are there to help (particularly senior men) is that "emotions are not some soft fluffy things that women feel" (as one client said!) They are a combination of all the chemical, biophysical, mechanical, and energetic factors your body makes in response to its environment and the brain's interpretation of what is happening. This cocktail can then lead your brain-body to conclude you are "feeling" something.

Professor Antonio Damasio has pointed out that it is possible have this e-motion, this energy in motion, and be unaware of what you are feeling.[49] Interestingly, research shows that men and women experience similar levels of e–motions. The difference between the sexes is that women tend to have greater conscious awareness of the emotions so they have more feelings. This awareness can lead to superior performance. Having an emotion without awareness means you will be unaware of the impact it has on your thinking and behaviour. This makes you vulnerable to the prevailing emotions you are experiencing. This is unlikely to lead to your best performance.

The Real Meaning of Soft Skills

This unwillingness to explore emotions at work has a number of causes. One of the first is the meaning we now give to the phrase *soft skills* which is used to describe things like emotional intelligence, active listening, influencing people, empathy and building rapport. This is in contrast to hard skills such as finance. The skills you need to succeed in turbulent environments are mostly soft skills.

Today, the *soft* in *soft skills* has been taken on the meaning of "*easy*" as in, "*This is a soft (easy) target.*" This doesn't make any sense as soft skills are usually much harder to develop than hard skills like finance. Hard skills suggest they are difficult when most hard skills are relatively straight forward. So what is the real meaning of soft and hard in this context?

Well, another meaning of "*soft*" is *malleable* like water. We could describe water as soft, fluid, and adaptable. Water adapts to its environment as it moves on its way. There's inherent flexibility in it. So when you think you have understood it, it can change form, going from water to ice or to steam. Consequently, it is difficult to offer a solid, unchanging definition. The definition is context–specific to some extent.

The "*hard*" in "*hard skills*" originally referred not to difficulty, but to solidity or rigidity. A rule of finance or physics *tends* to remain the same. Rock is hard. So instead of a choice between easy and difficult, it's really a choice between flexible/malleable and rigid/solid.

When we look at extreme situations, we see the artificial nature of this choice. At the extremes, many of the "rules" of physics turn out to be malleable. And the research in *Leadership in Dangerous Situations* show that being rigid about certain things such as values, trust and integrity (which are often perceived as "*soft*"), generates the most stable teams whose stability allows them to be more adaptable than the situation.

It would be easy for me to go overboard in praise of softness to counteract the distorted view that has emerged when people have taken the wrong meaning for soft and hard skills.[50] However, we want a combination of the two. Athletes need hardness that comes from muscle strength. But to use it effectively, they need flexibility and adaptability. In business, we need both too. I'd like to explore that combination in more detail now.

Confusing Activation with Performance

People often confuse activation with performance—as if there was some optimal level of activation for a stressor at work. Imagine you had a presentation to senior colleagues; would you want to be relaxed (low activation) or nervous (high activation)? Which is best? On a vertical line of increasing activation as you move to the top, which level would generate your optimal performance?

It's hard to answer it fully, isn't it? I can only answer this when I factor in your emotional state and the degree to which you are focusing on what's possible (being positive) vs. worrying about what could go wrong (being negative). Is it progress? So with our presentation, the key determinant would be whether you are seeing it as an opportunity or as a threat.

This brings us back to winning and losing and the Progress Principle. If we are winning, the high adrenalin and the positive growth hormones generate confidence and excitement. With the latter, the same level of adrenalin (activation) and a negative focus stimulates cortisol (a catabolic hormone designed to break something down). This cocktail would leave you anxious, worried, or even fearful.

What your brain and body decide will determine (and to some extent be determined by) the hormonal balance in your body. This determines the subsequent emotions, which obviously impacts on your behaviour. It's these emotions that play a truly pivotal role in how successful you are in dealing with the events that happen. Imagine being excited about the presentation–what will we be seeing? How about if you were anxious? The source of our answer to the optimal level of activation is on the horizontal axis which shows the degree to which we have a positive focus and anabolic state (building) or a negative focus and a catabolic state (breaking down).

So mapping a variety of emotional labels on our quadrants, we find a series of different emotional states.

Figure 8. The Stress Response and Emotions

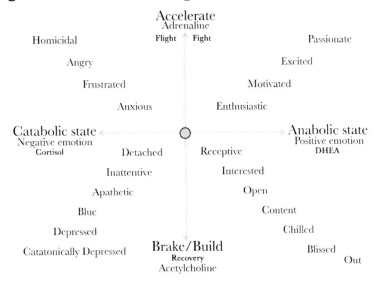

At the top left, high levels of adrenaline and cortisol stimulate strongly negative emotions, including anxiety, frustration, and anger. If you have lower negative activation, you are experiencing things like inattention, apathy, and depression. In your body, we will see high cortisol and low adrenalin.

Moving over to the right—low activation with hormones like DHEA (an anabolic hormone)—we have receptivity, interest, and openness. These are great emotional states for starting something. At the bottom quadrant, we have chilled or blissed out. Moving further up the positive side, we find energized, motivated, excited, even passionate emotions—the kinds of emotions that organizations most want from their people.[51]

Bringing It All Together

Let's look at this model again and instead of focusing on the emotions, look at the behaviours you may demonstrate if you were in different parts of the quadrants.

Thinking of the presentation example, imagine you saw this as an opportunity to prove yourself or to celebrate the great work your people had been doing. As we prepare for it, we are likely to feel some combination of appreciation, openness, and receptivity to what is happening. You'll be building momentum and, as you approached the presentation, you'd enjoy sharper concentration and be focused on the future possibilities and be excited and confident. This emotional combination will give you an additional bonus of another neurotransmitter called dopamine. This helps your brain to be creative. In fact, research shows that you can't be creative without a positive state as you only get dopamine from positive emotions.

If you were dreading the presentation, and perceived it as a threat, you may start off low in energy, demotivated, and perceiving a lack of challenge. As the negative pressure increased, the adrenalin and cortisol would increase causing you to become tense, restless, and pessimistic about the event and your prospects. You'd be more likely to snap at people and you may find it hard to focus. You would be preoccupied with what could go wrong and worried about any negative consequences.

Figure 9. Behavioural Expression of Emotions

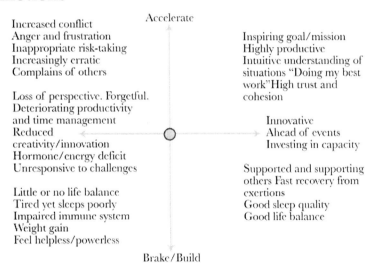

Increased conflict
Anger and frustration
Inappropriate risk-taking
Increasingly erratic
Complains of others

Loss of perspective. Forgetful.
Deteriorating productivity
and time management
Reduced
creativity/innovation
Hormone/energy deficit
Unresponsive to challenges

Little or no life balance
Tired yet sleeps poorly
Impaired immune system
Weight gain
Feel helpless/powerless

Accelerate

Inspiring goal/mission
Highly productive
Intuitive understanding of
situations "Doing my best
work" High trust and
cohesion

Innovative
Ahead of events
Investing in capacity

Supported and supporting
others Fast recovery from
exertions
Good sleep quality
Good life balance

Brake/Build

Recall what you do in day to day situations and your work so far on your stress curves. The typical transition from performing well to over activated and then suffering a drop in performance would see you moving from middle right to top right and then over to the left as your performance was negatively affected by stress.

What can you do to generate the performance states that are most helpful to you and to retreat from the ones you don't want? When you find yourself on the left, how do you refocus negative energy—what do you do to get back into neutral where you're in control of your thinking and can still influence your stress response?

Embrace the Challenge: Do Nothing Well

A key ability we need more and more in turbulent situations is the ability to *do nothing well.* My brother, Jason, first introduced me to this concept some years ago. He told me one day, *"You know Jon, I have realised that I don't do nothing well."* Thinking at first he had made a grammatical error (I can be a special kind of educated dumb at times), I asked him what he meant. He explained,

"I find it impossible to simply sit still—to do nothing well. I have to be doing something and it's not helpful."

My brother's idea is much more active than it sounds. Being able to first do nothing well allows you to temporarily inhibit what may be an instinctive fear driven reaction. This could keep your mind clear enough to think rapidly through your options. This helps your thinking to quickly catch up with the situation. Once up to speed, you will be able to focus on what's possible, make a decision and act.

The ability to do nothing before responding fully to a stressor gives you the best chance of ensuring your adaptation takes you up and to the right (accelerated heart rate and more adrenaline leading to improved concentration and increased energy) and avoiding the left quadrants which stimulate a much longer lasting stress response. Going up (and preferably to the right to meet a challenge) will give you a much quicker recovery. (This is the phasic adaptation I mentioned in an earlier chapter.)

Figure 10. Generating Optimal Emotional States

Increase Awareness of Self and Situation.

Fast Recovery

Regaining Perspective

Refuelling

Improving Sleep

Regaining Sense of Control

Strengthen the Core (PNS)

Emotional Management

Nutrition

Movement/Exercise

Respiration/Physical Connection

Staying Focused and Energised and at Your Best

Improving Perspective Getting Ahead of Events

Gaining and Giving Support

Life Balance

Improve Braking and Acceleration. Move to the Right

It's Hard To Do Nothing Well

This central grey box in the figure above is your support system—your daily PNS. The more work you do to strengthen your core, the greater your ability to handle challenging situations and ensure they stay right rather than go left. To return to the Prius metaphor, by strengthening your core, you will build more powerful batteries. This will allow you to tackle bigger stressors without really engaging the SNS. As energy comes in from the external situation, you need the strength to hold it and then have the flexibility to move to the side as you understand what is going on. So what do you do there to maintain your energy, oxygenation, emotional control, and so on?

The rest of the book is really about how to strengthen this core and how to think clearly under pressure. However, I would like to focus one last time on the initial stress response and the difference between phasic and tonic activation. Remember, we have approximately two minutes to recover sufficiently from a stressor to minimise any unnecessary responses in the body (this is the time it takes for cortisol to kick in).

What to Do in the First Two Minutes

We want to behave appropriately for the situation so we need to maintain the quality of our thinking. To do that, we need emotional control. And to get that we need to influence our physiology (our emotions being the sum of our physiological responses). Research (such as the work of Professor Damasio or the Institute of Heart Math) shows that our behaviour, thinking, emotions, and physiology are all interlinked. There is no a simple causal chain. Change any one and you change the others. However, if you can influence your physiology, you can reduce the main energy sources of unhelpful emotional responses.

I said earlier that this part of the body (controlled by the lower parts of the brain) is largely autonomous and automatic. But even though we can't control our physiology, we can influence it. And the crucial time for this is just before and then during the first few minutes of a stressful event. There is a relatively simple way to stop or even curtail this process of longer activation—we need to influence the beating of our hearts. I will explain how you can do that in the next chapter.

Summary

- Emotions are *energy-in-motion* and they play a key role in ensuring we respond helpfully to the challenges we face. Because of their energetic role, we can map different emotions to the different combinations of stress hormones.

- Which emotions we experience depends on whether we see something as a threat or a challenge, or whether we are likely to lose or win or to stall or make progress.

- If we have a strong core (PNS), we can cultivate the ability to do nothing well. That is, we are sufficiently strong to hold the energy, inhibit any instinctive physiological response that may not be suitable for our environment, and choose what to do instead.

- Success in this area begins with our ability to influence our stress response in the first two minutes of a challenge. If we can start well, the situation is likely to finish well.

7.

How to Change the Beating of Your Heart

Earlier, I explained how your internal emotionally driven response is far more significant in stress terms than the actual event itself. The simple skills described in this chapter will give you the capability to quickly achieve much deeper levels of core emotional stability. It will also give you one of the best ways I know to reactivate your PNS after a stressful experience. With practice, you will be able to dramatically reduce the duration of the stress response. This chapter is about the heart of stress leadership. I will explain how the insights from a small group of innovative scientists can give you a greater sense of control in your life and improve the functioning of your whole system.

Evolving Views of Our Hearts

Not very long ago, the prevailing view in Western medicine was that the heart was just an exquisitely designed mechanical pump whose sole purpose was to pump a fluid around a closed, unvented system. This contrasts with the literary or metaphorical view of the heart, which describes it as the centre of our emotions and even the seat of our soul. This "at the *heart* of things" view is present in just about every culture around the world. Many Eastern cultures still give the heart this predominance or at least equality with the mind in medicine too.

Medicine's Biggest Progress Trap

This Western separation of mind and body, and the related idea that the mind controls our emotions can be traced back to Rene Descartes and a deal he struck that made possible many of the amazing medical and scientific advances of the past 300 years.

To test his scientific ideas, Rene Descartes needed to dissect human bodies. To do that (and stay alive), he needed permission from the Catholic Church. After some resistance, Descartes made an agreement with the Pope. In exchange for permission to explore human anatomy, he had to limit his exploration the parts of the body and not look for anything that could refute the Church's teaching.

The safest way to do this was to study everything in isolation. Consequently, a dotted line was drawn between the mind and the body and a clear line between the spirit and everything else. Descartes famously pronounced *"I think, therefore I am"* and Western science took an enormous leap forward. (I confess to simplifying some steps here!)

This deal which really seemed like a good idea at the time created a brain centric approach to medicine where everything was primarily studied in isolation. To understand something, it is helpful to see things separately. The advances that came from understanding each discrete part of the human body were stunning. However, seeing things as separate in complex systems (and not just studying them separately) creates significant issues. In complex systems, relationships are often more important than the individual parts.

It's crucial after analysis to devote equal or greater time to synthesis or to reintegrate our new understanding into the picture of the whole. This new insight allows us to re-examine the relationships between the parts. A failure to do so can lead to even bigger problems as it creates expertise in separate fields but no one to draw the bigger, more important picture of how everything relates to and affects each other.

Today, especially with the deeper understanding and appreciation of systems and subtle interactions, the scientific view is coming much closer to the metaphorical view. Scientists such as Dr Candace Pert, Professor Antonio Damasio, The Institute of Heart Math, Dr Herbert Benson and Professor Stephen Porges are removing the artificial separation between mind and body.

We now know that the heart, in addition to interacting with the rest of the body biophysically (through pressure waves that you feel as your pulse) has three other known forms of communication with the rest of the body. It communicates and interacts neurologically (through the nervous system), biochemically (through hormones and neuro-transmitters), and energetically (especially magnetically and electromagnetically).

And, the heart, representing the body, effectively forms a tag team with the limbic brain that can easily overpower our thinking brains when it sees the need. I put the limbic (emotional centre) brain with the heart and not with the neo-cortex as its functions and cellular construction places it much closer to the body.

Some interesting things you may not know about the heart.

- **Your heart is 'older' than your brain.**
During conception, the heart actually forms before the brain. Scientists don't know the "intelligence" that instructs it to do so or how it does it, but the heart emerges creating its own networks around the body.

- **It has its own semi-autonomous nervous system** (which began during conception). All these things place it literally and metaphorically at the centre of things.

- **The heart can produce its own hormones.** It can make its own adrenaline, a chemical called ANF (atrial natriuretic factor), which regulates your blood pressure, and oxytocin, the "love peptide" or "bonding hormone," which is emitted during moments of connection, most notably with a mother and her baby when she is breast feeding.

- **The heart also plays a key role in how we become aware of a potential threat.** To answer the "*new/not new...threat/no threat*," questions, the amygdala communicates with the heart to get the body's assessment on how big a threat it senses. Heart beats seem to act as a summary of the body's assessments of what is happening. In the moments when a threat is recognised, the rhythm of the heart becomes temporarily incoherent. This incoherence jolts the rest of the system into action. This communication between the amygdala and the heart continues throughout the process. Most communication travels from the heart to the brain.

The Importance of Incoherent and Coherent Heart Signals

In the previous paragraph, I mentioned that the heart sends an *incoherent* heart beat through the body when it senses a potential threat. I am going to explain what I mean by that as it is crucial for the next part of your stress leadership development.

The focus for most people in assessing stress levels is in the increase in the number of beats per minute (bpm). Undoubtedly, an increased heart beat is a factor in preparing you for battle. *In theory*, the faster your heart rate, the more blood can be pumped around your system, the more prepared you are to fight that tiger. I say "in theory" because there's another factor that influences the amount of blood that gets pushed around your body. This is called heart rate variability (HRV).

Heart Rate Variability

If your heart is running at 60 beats per minute (bpm), what is it logical to think is the time between each beat? Sixty bpm would be one beat per second, right? Perfectly logical and wrong, except for when you are about to suffer a certain type of cardiac episode.[52] The space between each heart beat is actually changing all the time. This is called heart rate variability.[53]

The most important thing about your heart beat and your heart rate is not the number of beats per minute but the rhythm and pattern between each beat. As you breathe in, the gap may be one that starts you off at 60 beats a minute and then goes up to a 70 beat average, then 80, and 90 and then drop back as we exhale.

When you're experiencing positive emotions (and feeling safe) such as feeling energized and engaged, the pattern or oscillation in your heart beats mirror a wave moving smoothly up and down (called a sinusoidal wave). When you're stressed, anxious, or frustrated (and feeling threatened) the pattern will be incoherent. This is a key variable the brain considers as it assesses a situation. An incoherent rhythm accelerates the stress response. The incoherent communication coming from the heart (biophysical, neurological, biochemical, and energetic) reduces energy intensive conscious thought and prepares you for intense, physical activity (battle).

The variability in your heart beat affects the way the additional power is applied from your heart. When stressed and incoherent, your heart rate and blood pressure can increase but the blood transported through the system can hardly increase at all because of the incoherent rhythm–the worst of both worlds. [As an analogy, compare the difference between smooth, controlled acceleration in a car and erratically slamming your foot on and off the accelerator.]

If you can engage in intense physical activity when you receive this incoherent signal, this type of response would be fantastic. Your heart gives your system a jolt to help your brain to register the threat and the incoherent signal quickly becomes more coherent as you start to run or fight.

By standing still, though, (while you're listening to your boss/client tell you off about something), your heart registers the lack of movement (or fighting) and assumes there has been a breakdown in communication. So it turns up the volume and gives you more incoherence. If this happens enough you can contract *viral stupidity* and lose the ability to think. The communication from the heart shuts down your neo–cortex to prepare you for fight/flight.

In today's workplace setting, this temporary loss of brain power tends to make your boss/client even angrier as you have nothing intelligent to say. Once this incoherence has established itself you are only a minute or so away from the cortisol response and a much longer stress curve. If only wrestling was a legitimate form of conflict resolution at work, you'd be fine!

So what can you do? Well, triggering a positive emotion would stimulate a more coherent, supportive rhythm. However, that's tricky to begin with (rather like asking a first time sprinter to run an 11-second 100m). Fortunately, there is something mechanical you can do. It's relatively easy, and it's something you are already doing–breathing. Changing the pattern of your breathing can allow you to influence your system enough to keep thinking. This gives you the best chance of doing something constructive to get you back over to the right-hand quadrants.

Why "Taking a Deep Breath" Can Help

No doubt if you have found yourself in a tough situation, someone has reminded you to *"Take a deep breath,"* or, "C*ount to ten."* This sometimes helps, doesn't it? Have you ever thought why? When I ask this, many clients point to the increased oxygen coming into your system. This does help but the biggest reason is actually more fundamental.

Huygen's Pendulum

Taking a deep breath and/or counting (rhythmically) tends to have a calming influence due to something called entrainment. Entrainment is a concept from physics discovered by Dutchman Christiaan Huygens. Huygens invented the pendulum clock. Once he'd invented the second pendulum clock, he found that two pendulums, when placed closely together, tended to establish the same pendulum swing and became synchronised or entrained with each other. This phenomenon of systems or organisms become aligned and entrained is common in nature, and it's something that happens in the body.

Through the process of entrainment–of one organ mirroring the actions of its neighbour–you can positively affect heart function to reduce stress and improve effectiveness. The lungs effectively hug the heart so if such a large organ as the lungs has a coherent rhythm (moving in and out steadily), it affects the heart and calms the incoherence. This means your heart's incoherence can be reduced if you breathe rhythmically.

This is worth doing for a number of reasons. Firstly, you will probably be able to maintain your core balance long enough to think through how to satisfy your boss/client or whichever stressor is affecting you. This limits the size of the unnecessary aspects of the stress response and flattens other physiological responses, thereby giving you other health benefits such as reduced blood pressure, etc. Breathing rhythmically also could improve the effectiveness of your blood circulating around your body as the acceleration of your pulse would not be hindered by incoherent heart beats.

"Take a Rhythmical, Patterned Breath..."

To recap then, it's not so much the depth of your breath that calms you but that fewer, slower breaths tend to be more rhythmical than lots of short, shallow ones. I admit that, "*Take a rhythmical breath*," is not as catchy – especially with small children–but that is what the science tells us to do. Let's look more closely at what the science suggests?

1. **Establish a basic rhythm.** Complete a full breath–in and out–in a consistent time, say every eight or 10 seconds. The in and out stages are split evenly (e.g. in for four or five seconds, out for four or five seconds). Some studies suggest that a resting adult male breathing at six breaths a minute tends to generate one of the best power outputs of the heart. This combines maximum variability with readiness for action. So if you are an adult male who happens to be resting, try this yourself.

Remember that you want to be able to breathe rhythmically at any time, even when exercising. This means you need to be able to vary the rhythm. More important is to experiment to see what works best for you. You're breathing will be just right if you find your mind clearing and if you feel at ease. You'll know if you're breath is too deep if you start to feel light headed (you are taking in too much oxygen).

2. **Focus on a smoother pattern.** A common recommendation from activities like yoga is to have two seconds of out-breath for every one second of in-breath so if you're breathing in for three seconds, breathe out for six seconds or in for four and out for eight. Dr Stephen Porges highlights through his polyvagal theory that SNS activation is on the in-breath where your pulse quickens. PNS recovery is activated during the out-breath and your pulse drops back. By my limited understanding of his work, the one to two ratio would allow more space for recovery, which would be useful if you wanted to reduce the level of activation in your system. If you wanted to maintain the activation but make it more coherent and positive, keep the in and out breath the same and then change your focus of attention.

3. **Change your focus of attention.** The Institute of Heart Math recommend that (as you breathe in a rhythmical, patterned way) you can increase effectiveness further by moving your attention to your heart. And as you are breathing, imagine you are breathing through your heart and think of something positive, such as someone or something you appreciate. This sounds a little strange, so practice it before trying it in a stressful situation. It does have an excellent effect of clearing your mind.

We will come back to this in the care and support section when we focus on activating positive emotions. For now though, just try it and see what happens. It's important to cultivate positive emotions as the heart's erratic beating will soon overwhelm any attempts to breathe rhythmically if the stress persists. When you experience positive emotions your heart produces a coherent rhythm. This rhythm literally sends coherence around your entire body via the waves the heart emits—the most obvious being physical pulse waves. The positive emotion generates coherence which helps you to feel safe.

Something to Practice Every Day

Regulating your breathing has such an impact on maintaining your core emotional stability, it's often one of the first things I start with when helping new clients. This also makes the more important task of cultivating positive emotions much easier as you start from further over to the right on the four quadrants.

To practice, start with a minimum of three quiet periods of five or 10 minutes a day. Begin to focus on improving the rhythm of your breathing, then the pattern, then your focus. Slowly reduce the need for you to look at your watch by first counting along and then just following the sensation in your chest and the rest of your body. After a short while, say a week or two, start doing it when completing a repetitive activity that requires little thought—your morning commute on the train, when exercising, or even periodically in meetings for example. You will quickly be able to approximate the pattern so you will no longer need to look at a watch or even count in your head.

Then begin doing it more and more as you go about your day. I have found it useful for exercising and research shows it maximises available oxygen in your body (below maximal threshold). Exercising tends to go better (improved performance and faster recovery-from my experience), and you have a prolonged period of coherent breathing during your day. This can increase overall coherence and maximises the positive benefit of the exercise. Eventually you will have sufficient awareness and control to take a few seconds to establish a pattern and then get on with your work. Soon, a couple of deliberate, rhythmical breaths will begin to immediately activate more coherent HRV as that will become your default pattern. This means you will be able to establish a coherent pattern almost at will so it can help you be more present at important times and quickly reactivate your PNS after a stressful engagement.

Helping a Stressed, Pregnant Friend

A few years ago, I was catching up on the phone with an entrepreneur friend who was 35 weeks pregnant. She was finding it impossible to switch off as she had so much work to hand over to her team before having her baby. She was sleeping for only three to four hours a night. Given how far advanced her pregnancy was (and just how hard those first few months are as a new parent), I suggested we meet immediately.

I introduced her to the Heart Math software and the techniques I have just described in this chapter. They seemed to help. Given the urgency, we agreed to speak the next day to review her progress. The next day she didn't ring at the allotted time, which was the first time she had ever failed to make an engagement. When we finally spoke some hours later, she explained:

> *"Well, the traffic was light all the way home so I managed to count my breathing in and out for most of the journey. I did it before going to bed and as I prayed. I was amazed that I slept for 7 hours. Before our call, I decided to do another 10 minutes so I made myself comfortable in an arm chair and focused on my breath and I woke up two hours later!"*

US Special Forces

The head of Research for the Institute of Heart Math, Dr Rollin McCraty, works a great deal with US Armed Forces. The techniques go down especially well in that environment as everything can be tested. Here's what one Special Forces operative had to say about coherence during a combat situation.

> I learned coherence while in sniper school as a Special Forces operative. I practiced on a daily basis because of the many benefits it offered beyond just job performance. One situation that stands out the most for me is when I was deployed with my unit [for combat operations.]
>
> On one of our daily patrols we found ourselves under intense fire by heavily armed combatants. During this stressful combat situation I was able to automatically achieve a coherent state...This resulted in a much greater operational awareness that allowed me to confidently and accurately orchestrate our maneuver while in a mind-body state than can only be described as serene. I found that the more coherent I became during this situation the more my unit emulated my relaxed confident demeanor. They trusted me and my decisions, and the cohesion was stronger than it had ever been before.
>
> After that, we began practicing performance improvement and control techniques, including coherence training, as a team. This greatly enhanced our overall capability and readiness in our duties and quality of life. I strongly believe that the continuous practice of using the coherence techniques as part of a proactive preparation strategy has literally saved my life and others around me.[54]

I think this example demonstrates just how quickly you can deactivate a stress system if you know exactly what to do and if you have prepared for the challenge you are facing. It is also a great example of how a coherent leader and a committed team can navigate an extraordinarily hostile physical environment through the creation of a safe social environment. Rhythmical, patterned breathing focused on the heart can make an enormous difference if you are willing to do the work.

Buy the emWave Stress Relief System

If you would like to take this further, I suggest buying some books from the Heart Math Institute. They have a series of short books that help you transform specific emotional states such as anger, stress, and anxiety. Find the book that relates to your most challenging emotional state and transform it through daily practice. Another book to explain the science of cardiac coherence and HRV is *Healing Without Freud or Prozac* by Dr David Servan–Schreiber. The two chapters he devotes to the topic are superb and the rest of the book is excellent.

If you have the budget, then buy the emWave Stress Relief Desktop Software or an App for your smartphone. This gives you direct feedback on the impact you are having on your HRV. It's an excellent tool and gives you immediate, clear evidence of the progress you are making.

Even though we can't control our physical response we can influence it massively–if you are willing to do the work. As a way to limit the amount of unhelpful acceleration in the short term, I have found this practice to be the best I know.

Simply breathing differently will not eliminate all stressed reactions. Saying that would be akin to saying if you do some weight training you'll be able to lift anything. Sometimes our internal incoherence is so great we can't stop the momentum until we have done something we regret. We all have a breaking point. The long term gain comes from combining it with a positive focus (step three of the process) and from strengthening your whole system. We are devoting a whole chapter developing more helpful emotional states at the end of the book. And the next chapter will help you to strengthen your whole system.

Summary

- The prevailing assumption in Western medicine for a long time has been that the heart and body are subordinate to the brain. This is factually incorrect.
- The heart summarises the body's understanding of what is happening in its environment and communicates this to the brain.
- At times, signals from the body and heart can override those of the neo–cortex.
- What matters most for a helpful stress response is not your heart rate (beat per minute) but your heart rhythm and the degree to which it is coherent or incoherent. Coherence denotes safety, incoherence danger.
- We cannot control out heart beat but we can influence it by breathing rhythmically so the lungs guide the heart through the process of entrainment.
- If practiced regularly, and combined with work on positive emotions, this can give you the opportunity to minimise the stress response sufficiently that you will be able to generate more positive emotions and have fewer stress responses. Emotions create much deeper patterns of coherence in the body.
- Strive for coherence whenever you can. The creation of a default coherent pattern gives you a much

greater sense of personal control which helps to keep you within sustainable or stretch bands.

8.
Accumulate and Attract Resources

The last chapter gave you a clearer sense of how performance and emotions (energy–in–motion) can be used to generate winning responses. The chapter also concluded our work that focused on mastering the moment–optimising our response to discrete acute stressors. This focus on the first ABC of stress and success [improve Acceleration and Braking and reduce Cost] minimises the chance of suffering the type of chronic stress caused by a chain of acutely stressful events with insufficient resources for recovery.

The remainder of the book will be focused on the second ABC of stress and success. This will help you to adapt (and thrive) for 0–90 days. To quickly remind ourselves of this ABC, they are:

1. **Accumulate and attract resources** to improve your capacity and capability for handling turbulence.

2. **Brain Function**–Support and structure your thinking so that you can maintain perspective, deepen your environmental awareness, think clearly, and avoid "progress traps."

3. **Care and Support**–Ensure you get (and give) the help and support needed for you and those you care about to tackle the challenges ahead.

Our focus in this chapter is accumulating and attracting resources but you can start wherever you prefer.. This will strengthen your PNS (your core) and will reduce your fixed stress costs. As we have explored at length, the fight-flight stress response that we activate so frequently causes unnecessary and unsustainable wear and tear on our bodies. Almost as importantly, the very same short term stress focus ("Just get through today!") causes us to neglect the activities that could minimise and even eliminate much of that wear and tear.

My aim in this chapter is to offer you ways to reduce this wear and tear by strengthening your core. This will add more detail to the ideas in chapter six. A stronger core gives you the ability to choose where you are on the four quadrants in tougher situations without triggering the deeper tonic activation. Tonic activation leads to the excessive cortisol production we so want to avoid. Here is the diagram from chapter six again.

Figure 10. Generating Optimal Emotional States

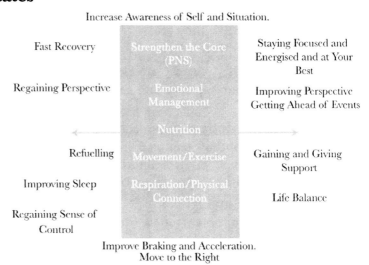

Our first principle of leading our physical response to stress is to improve the quality of our breathing. This aids our recovery and helps us to maintain our core stability. This will help a lot, but it still won't be enough to keep us safe in our chronically stressful environment. What will keep us safe is the focus of this chapter.

The research on performance in challenging situations makes a clear link between physical fitness and wellbeing and the time it takes to catch viral stupidity. Fitness doesn't make you smarter but it does inoculate you to some extent from many of the stress–induced cognitive errors we can experience. If you want to handle more turbulence, strengthen your PNS core and a key part of that is your physical fitness.

So we are going to look at the following areas:

a) Movement and exercise
b) Food and drink
c) Sleep, rest and recovery

Of all the chapters in this book, it is this one in which I may sound most like your gran. I would be surprised if much of the information in this chapter was new to you. This isn't an apology just a quick heads up of what to expect. If you wrote down all the things you used to do to take care of yourself (but stopped), I would guess you will see most of them here. This isn't rocket science and most is really simple. But as Peter Drucker used to say, if it isn't simple, it won't work. This works. All you have to do is work at it.

8a.
Movement and Exercise

There are three main goals I encourage my clients to aim for with movement and exercise. In order of priority, these are:

1. Recover faster
2. Avoid injury by increasing flexibility and balanced strength
3. Increase capacity

Use the Energy Your Body Has Created

The stress response produces energy to tackle what it assumes to be a physical stressor. Where possible, use this energy on the day you create it. Going to the gym may help but it isn't my first suggestion on how to use it. You are likely to get better, sustained results by simply increasing the level of physical activity throughout your day. A series of short periods of movement lasting five- to 15-minute will help you to use most of the energy, stay calmer and take your activation back to normal. You can do most of this by simply changing how you do some necessary activities.

Increase Movement During Your Day

Walk quickly between meetings or get out of the lift at an earlier floor and walk the rest of the way. Do the same when using public transport. I work in London and it is sometimes quicker to walk between stations than it is to travel on the underground. So explore options in your environment to see if this increased movement can actually save you time as you reduce stress.

Persuade colleagues to join you. Walk to a new café or even have a walking meeting—this needs to be one where you don't need to worry about detailed minutes! And it helps to remain connected with your external environment. So a walk through a park will give you a deeper sense of harmony than running in a gym. This walking, combined with rhythmical breathing, can reactivate your PNS and really put on the brakes of your stress response.

During meetings, encourage people to move and to take regular mobile phone free breaks of two-five minutes every 90 minutes. You'll notice a performance improvement. Also, tense your stomach muscles frequently when seated. This keeps you sitting upright, minimises back problems, and gives you some exercise.

Try "Work Hard, Play Easy"

Of the three main priorities for movement and exercise, the first two, recover faster and avoid injury, are most important. Capacity building is a distant third in turbulent times. It often takes two to three months to get to when working with new clients.

If you have a tough job and don't already exercise at least three times a week, avoid strenuous exercise completely. Intense activity, when you don't already have a reasonable level of fitness, is more likely to lead to injuries or illness than to help. This is because you will be using resources needed for recovery. Rest is sometimes more important than movement. That's why I advise my clients to "*work hard, play easy.*"

I appreciate that this could sound weak in cultures where you are encouraged to "*Eat Stress!*" Remember, you don't eat stress, stress eats you! And this is what the research recommends. Regardless of it looking weak, it is actually the best way to stay strong. I apply this principle myself and I am the strongest I have ever been.

Mark Allen, the Ironman triathlete who was recently voted by ESPN viewers as the greatest endurance athlete of all time, attributed much of his success to the low activation, endurance training he did at the start of each year. Until surprisingly late in pre–season, Allen never allowed his heart rate to go above 150bpm.[55] He also said that many of his opponents' injuries were probably caused by their overtraining and pushing too hard early in the season.

Move Without Breaking a Sweat

In practice, this *play easy* approach will give you a heart rate during exercise of 50% to 70% of your maximum suggested heart rate. (To get a rough idea of your maximum heart rate take 220 and subtract your age). At this rate (e.g.110–120 bpm) you may be able to exercise without breaking a sweat. This means you could go for a brisk walk for 20 minutes at lunch on your way to the cafe, and you won't need a shower afterwards– great when time is short. And if you walk down the stairs instead of using the lift, you can include that in the time too. After a couple of such walks every week, you can then start to do more challenging sessions when your energy levels allow.

The only exception to this play easy principle is after a really tough day where you are so stressed (and perhaps angry) you need to burn up a massive amount of energy or you won't get to sleep. The ideal time for this kind of work–out is late afternoon (between 3.30pm to 5pm). This means you can exercise hard without the stimulating effect of exercise inhibiting sleep. Just be sure to warm up and cool down properly. You can also go back to work for a couple of hours with a clear head if you need to.

To make this gentler exercise easier to do, buy a heart rate monitor–a cheap one is fine. Use it to ensure you are within a moderate bpm band. This keeps you safe

especially if you have the occasional overwhelm—
eliminating strenuous session.

Find an Exercise You Like With People You Like

To increase the likelihood of exercising, find an exercise you like and do it with people you like. Leading health expert, Leslie Kenton, points out that the negative stress of doing exercise under duress is likely to counteract the benefits of the movement. She says you must find the form of movement you enjoy. Then find your exercise tribe, i.e. other people with whom you can exercise. People will skip exercising on their own but will go if they know that someone is waiting at the gym.[56]

Remember that at these lower intensity levels, as long as you are moving, you can call anything exercise. So going to a dance class can be a fantastic way to speed up recovery. You also get a one hour focus on rhythm which can help to generate coherence.

Avoid Injury—Consider Yoga or Pilates

A great way to help you to recover and avoid injury is to take up some form of stretching practice, for example, yoga or Pilates. Brig Gen (Ret) Tom Kolditz, formally head of Behavioural Sciences and Leadership at West Point, makes this recommendation in his excellent book, *In Extremis Leadership*. He stresses the importance of three things in preventing injuries—joint stability, balance, flexibility. He says, "Probably the finest activity to hone and maintain balance and flexibility is yoga."[57]

The key thing is to choose exercise that promotes balance both literally and metaphorically. Hans Selye was adamant that no one ever dies of old age; they die because one part of their body has worn faster than all the others.[58] Athletes with unusually long careers nearly always have a much more proactive approach to injury prevention than average athletes. Two examples of this from the UK are soccer players, David Beckham and Ryan Giggs. Ryan Giggs made a DVD to show his yoga training regimen. Going to a class really helps you develop your technique but DVDs and video game versions also will help as you will be able to do them when you are away. Start gentle–getting injured doing yoga would be ironic and painful, but funny!

Increase Strength

On average we lose 1lb of muscle and add an extra lb. of fat every year from our late 20s. So we go from being strong and slim in our 20s to fat and weak in our 50s. This deterioration is so common that it is one of the best measures of your biological age. It is utterly reversible and totally unnecessary. It doesn't happen because we are getting old, it happens because we stop using our muscles. We get out of shape because of poor habits. It hardly ever has anything to do with getting older.

For clients in their 30s or 40s, I *recommend* strength work. For clients over 50, I *proactively encourage (nag)* and for clients over 60, I will *absolutely insist* on strength work. **At that age, you are too old not to do it!**

It makes such a difference to your physical health. Strength work leads to increased strength, better posture, fewer injuries, less fat as you burn more calories, and you look and feel better too. The key is to start steadily.

Also notice that I don't say "*lift weights.*" I use weights because I have them and I enjoy it. There are other ways. You can regain strength by using your own body as the force of resistance or by using bands (essentially large rubber bands). These other methods mean you can build strength at home or in your hotel room if you are working away.

Dr Charles Eugster 93-Year-Old Stud Muffin

As way of inspiration, be sure to Google the amazing Dr Charles Eugster, a body builder who happens to be 93 years old. He competed at Henley Rowing Regatta as a young man (in 1938!) He continued rowing all his life but, at 88 years young, Dr Eugster realised he was gaining fat and his muscles were wasting away. Being the proactive guy he is, he found a former Mr Universe and became the world's oldest body builder! He won 3 World Masters Gold medals at the age of 93, bringing his total to 35!

Increase Your Sense of Purpose

Sometimes your long-term health and well-being offers insufficient motivation to take care of yourself in the short term. If you are having trouble with motivation to do what you know is good for you, find a bigger purpose.

One thing I find works really well is to persuade your organisation to raise money for the CEO's favourite charity by doing a physical challenge. You can get everyone else involved in the office, and even your customers, all with CEO support. This makes taking the time to exercise much more acceptable.

When individual clients want to lose weight, I encourage them to commit to an endurance event six to 12 months in the future and collect money for a charity immediately. This tells everyone you care about that you are serious about losing weight and also can inspire them to do the same. It also gives you lots of reasons to stick to the plan.

If this is a little extreme for you (there is only one way out of it) find ways to move more and then to exercise in a way that you find enjoyable. The return on more movement quickly becomes positive through benefits such as improved sleep, clearer thinking, and faster recovery and increased resilience.

8b.
Food and Drink

Making more helpful food and drink choices is a great way to strengthen your core. Improvements can be fast and, like breathing, you are doing it anyway so why not do it just a little better?

Food and drink are supposed to strengthen our system yet many of our choices fail to give our bodies what we need to recover. They also create additional stress by adding processed, chemically suspect food product that our bodies find hard to digest. This means our food choices can inadvertently push ourselves into chronic stress.

The Anglo-American approach to food is the least healthy in the world as we tend to focus way too much on the transactional—just get the calories and individual nutrients. We don't focus enough on the relationship and the impact this food stuff will have on our bodies—where nutrients, chemicals, and quality are more important. And we prioritise quantity over quality. [Research into longevity suggests the single easiest thing to do to extend your life is to live on a slightly calorie restricted diet.]

Conduct Your Own Research Then Test It

There are some excellent authors in this area (and quite a few poor ones!) Read a few and then make your own mind through testing. It does take time to begin with but you have such a clear sense of what does and doesn't work for you that you can quickly see through the latest diet fad and focus back on what you know works. The most important lesson I took from my physical recovery was to strengthen the relationship and communication I have with my body. This will help you improve your relationship with your body.

Two authors I really like are Michael Pollan and Leslie Kenton. Even though Leslie's most recent book in this area was published more than 10 years ago (*Age Power* in 2002), don't be put off. I'll take 10-year-old Kenton wisdom over just about anyone else's wisdom. She researches extremely well, writes eloquently and she has also been promoting healthy living since the 1970s. Then everyone dismissed her as a crazy but entertaining American. Tellingly, most of her "*crazy*" suggestions are now considered mainstream.

Michael Pollan offers great, easy to follow advice. I first read *In Praise of Food* but have since come across *Food Rules*.[59] This book is the most elegant book about good eating I have ever seen. Pollan's recommendations include the following:

- Eat food, not food product
- Avoid food products containing ingredients that an 8 year-old child couldn't pronounce.
- If it came from a plant, eat it: if it was made in a plant, don't.
- Pay more, eat less.
- Cook and, if you can, plant a garden.

His core argument is that knowing what to eat is actually simple. The essential challenge we face is that the Western diet comprising refined starchy carbohydrates, refined sugars, man-made chemicals and fats, and lots of meat (with hardly any fruit, vegetables and whole grains) suits no one. I agree with him. I have seen no data to suggest you can eat our Western diet and stay well.

Pollan makes many of the same conclusions as fascinating book called *The Saccharine Disease* written by Dr T.L. Cleave in 1974. This followed a life time of research into the effects of removing fiber from our diets and eating refined sugar.[60] Cleave's research showed that any society that adopts the Western diet gets all the Western illnesses within 40 years. It's from Cleave's work that we all know we should eat fiber. The more you can remove refined food products such as refined sugars, starches, and chemicals from your diet, the less additional stress you will place on your body, the healthier you will be.

Don't worry about applying all the advice immediately. Try out a few of the ideas and see what results you get. To stress one more time: test, test, and test! Improve the quality of your choices further by applying more ideas when you are ready. Getting stressed because you have not been able to eat organically or avoid refined sugars increases stress. Make progressively healthier choices and focus on your powers of recovery.

General Principles

Meet today's needs and strengthen tomorrow. Reduce your need for the immediate, synthetic energy offered by coffee and sugary products just to get you through the day. Focus instead on eating the things that will meet that energy need and help strengthen your system.

Your body needs the nutrients in whole foods. Eat food whole with the minimum amount of processes. Many foods are marketed for one key additive or element. Fresh food contains so many helpful ingredients (many of them understood incompletely), it would be impossible to have just one marketing claim (e.g. for tomatoes or blueberries).

When choosing food, imagine a continuum beginning with raw, uncooked vegetables moving onto steamed or stir-fry, then more intensive cooking methods until you reach food product with increasingly sophisticated and unhelpful industrial processes. The far end of the scale would be microwaved ready meals. Stay as close to the raw end as you can.

Improve the Quality of What you Eat and Eat Less of It. Eat better quality food and eat less of it in total. Sometimes you may fancy some chocolate (often a sign you are low in magnesium). Instead of having a cheap bar with poor quality nutrients that leaves you wanting more, go for the best quality and simplest bar you can find, such as one with 70% plus cocoa. You'll have to practically force yourself to eat the whole bar (even I had to work at it!). If you go for great quality, traditional sources, you will need far less willpower to stop yourself eating all of it.

Choose Protein as a Vegan (if You Can). When choosing protein, look for appetising choices first as a vegan. If nothing attracts you, choose as a vegetarian. And if you still haven't found something, choose as a Thomas Jefferson inspired omnivore.

Practically, this means starting with raw seeds and nuts, then pulses, then good quality eggs (and some dairy), and finally meat. Also, explore which seeds and nuts suit you best. For some reason pumpkin seeds and pecan nuts work best with me. But everyone is different. Go easy starting out, though, as your body may take a while to get used to raw protein again.

Jefferson (quoted in Pollan) said "*Let meat be thy condiment.*" This have a meal of mainly vegetables with meat as an accompanying flavour—instead of indulging our modern habit of having a large steak with a lettuce leaf as garnish!

It's important to eat things willingly. If you are eating what you describe as "rabbit food" and really don't want to I'd suggest something less virtuous that you are happy eating and then get healthier foods when you are ready.

For portions, Leslie Kenton (in *Age Power*) suggests the "*palm rule*" for meat and vegetables. When deciding how much to have, eat a palm sized piece of meat and at least two palms of vegetables (as close to raw as is safe).[61]

Your body craves sugar, salt and fat when stressed – it does not crave junk food. Some of my clients tell me that they crave junk food when they are stressed. I know this feeling well as my diet was mostly junk food when I was in trouble. Deprived of adequate sleep with a weakened core, I would find energy from any food source that was sugary, salty, or fatty–what we would normally associate with junk food. I would then spend the rest of the day eating similar rubbish fighting the inevitable sugar drop.

That your body craves sweet, salty and fatty foods doesn't mean that your body craves junk food. Your body is asking for food that is high in easily accessible energy and stress chemical building blocks–i.e., sugary, salty, and fatty foods. It just happens that junk food is sugary, salty and fatty. What a coincidence!

Our bodies have a problem with junk food because the sugar, salt, and fat tend to be refined and none have the nutrients of the originals (and the chemicals in these foods add additional stress to your system). For example, with regard to wanting salty foods, you actually crave sodium (not salt), because that contains vital minerals your cells need to repair themselves when you have a prolonged exposure to stress.

Most salt today is simply industrially produced salty flavouring. The other 90 or so essential minerals found in real salt such as sea salt or rock salt, have been left out. Receiving the salty flavour without the minerals confuses your body and causes it to increase its demands for this flavour. This is why you find yourself being compelled to eat more and more rubbish.

If you do want a plate of fries then have your own supply of quality salt. This will limit the craving for even more as you'll get energy, a full stomach (which gives you a satisfied feeling for a little while), and the minerals.

If you find yourself in a stress–induced junk food rut, you can find yourself craving more and more. This can be due to the effect the fat has on certain receptors of the brain. The fat can produce a similar feeling to taking morphine. Given how good this feels, it can create what amounts to a moderate chemical addiction. So if you find that you have to have junk, then wean yourself off it for a few months until the cravings have gone. If you still need the energy (sugar and fat), choose sources your great-grandparents would have eaten.

Reduce starchy carbohydrate consumption. Your body needs protein and normal carbohydrates (vegetables) far more than it does starchy carbohydrates. If you still need some for energy, then eat starchy carbohydrates and proteins separately. This makes digestion easier.

On the choice of starchy carbohydrates, experiment to see which ones your body finds easiest to digest. As a general principle, go for the ones that require the least amount of processing before you can eat them. You will find your body will make its own suggestions if you listen carefully enough.

Reducing chemicals is more important than reducing fat. I was having dinner at a friend's house one night and was speaking of my love of Greek yoghurt. He was tucking in to *"healthy option"* fat free yoghurt. I asked him if he knew what replaced the fat. He didn't so he took a look. Compared to the ingredients of Greek yoghurt [*Contains: Milk*], the fat free yoghurt contained:

Yoghurt, Water, Banana Puree (3%), Fructose, Modified Starch, Inulin, Gelatine, Flavourings, Colours: Carotenes, Curcumin; Sweeteners: Aspartame, Acelsulfame K; Caramel syrup, Acidity Regulator: Citric Acid.

Are a few grams of fat really so bad that it's worth exposing yourself to all those chemicals—especially those that have been proven to be carcinogenic? Your body can handle animal fat much more easily than man-made chemicals. If you want to cut down fat, just eat less.

Eliminate artificial sweeteners and have less sugar of any kind. Talking of Aspartame, research the artificial sweeteners in the food you eat. Then decide what is best for you. Great alternatives to artificial sweeteners that are 100% natural are stevia and agave nectar. Stevia is a natural plant extract from the sunflower family. It was made available in the UK in 2012 and is now in some coffee shops. Agave nectar is a delicious tasting sweetener from the same plant used to make tequila. It looks like thin honey and is much sweeter, so you use less. It's fast acting so can help if you need some energy quickly, but it doesn't produce the drop in energy that comes from refined sugar. This is because it has a high natural fructose to glucose ratio, which gives it a lower glycaemic index. It's so good I use it as a booster fuel during triathlons.

Stop eating microwaved food. One of the most interesting conference speakers I have ever heard was the evolutionary biologist, Elisabet Sahtouris. At a conference in 2004, she stood up and one of the first things she said was "*Stop using a microwave!*" Her argument then was that microwaving food damages the molecules and its nutrients, so the food is less healthy. Our bodies just can't handle the maladapted molecules.

I was so impressed that I went home and tried to throw out our microwave. My wife stopped me but over the next six months we gradually reduced our need to have one (through better planning) and we threw it out.

Given how convenient the microwave is, I imagine you would be reluctant to do this. So do your own research. If a 10-minute Google search into "microwave dangers" doesn't cause you at least reduce its use, I'll stop pestering you. If you have small children and heat a lot of their food or milk in a microwave, please take 20 minutes. I promise it will be worth it.

If You Can't Be Good, Be Less Bad. One of the most valuable things I learned about food as an obese stress monkey was the stimulating effect that various junk foods had on my body. This was helpful as I returned to health as I knew which foods to stop eating. However, it continues to be useful when I am working away on a tight deadline and may be suffering from jet lag. I know exactly what I need to eat and drink to have just enough synthetic energy to deliver! I also know the consequences so I can plan for the recovery.

Learn which combination of sugary, fatty, and salty foods gets you through for the lowest cost you can minimise the necessary recovery when you need to get through a tough situation. Aim for better quality (or less bad) and try to have the protein and the fat without the starchy carbs (or eat fewer of those). And, if you can manage a few healthy choices along the way, such as water or freshly squeezed juice (preferably green), you will make the recovery easier when things calm down.

Drink

Drink enough water. Your body will welcome more water to help with the cleaning process and, if you are dehydrated, then you will see an immediate improvement by drinking more water. A good approximation for determining how much water to drink comes from Leslie Kenton. Take your weight in kilograms and divide it by 8. This will give you the number of 200ml glasses of water to take. If you are 80kg, then you will need 10 glasses (2l). This rule varies depending on the season and if you are exercising, but it's a good guideline. As with everything, test it. Just take in enough to pee every two hours or so.

Also focus on eating water rich foods more than processed foods. One of the biggest reasons why your body becomes dehydrated is that processed food has hardly any water in it and your body needs a lot of water to flush it out of your system.

Drink coffee like an Italian. If you want coffee, drink it like they do in Italy as often as you can. Have a small, but high-quality espresso and a glass of water. This Italian approach maximises the stimulant, minimises the recovery with the water offering immediate compensation for the dehydrating effects of the coffee. Don't have a pint of coffee flavoured milk you get in some coffee shops chains.

Avoid caffeine after lunch (unless you really need the stimulation). This gives your body a chance to get it out of your system before you go to bed. As a rule, one to three cups a day should be your max. If you do need to drink it, then get the best quality coffee you can afford and apply the Italian rule. This will reduce the actual amount you need and increase the effect when you need a boost.

Eliminate diet drinks and reduce carbonated drinks. If you are unsure, simply Google the ingredients of your favourite diet drink. And if you won't eliminate, half your consumption for a month, replacing it with water or herbal tea and review the results. A friend used to get headaches every afternoon and assumed it was overwork. She started drinking water instead of Diet Coke, and the headaches vanished immediately. She was simply dehydrated.

Drink herbal tea–especially green tea or white tea. Green tea is a healthy drink and it has a younger, fitter sibling: *white tea.*

Tea basics: black tea (the most common), green tea, and white tea can come from the same plants. The difference is when the leaves are picked and how much fermentation (preparation after picking) takes place. The earlier the leaves are picked in the growing season, and the less fermentation, the healthier the tea, the lighter it is. White tea gets its name from the small white hairs on the leaves as it is picked before the leaf has had chance to turn green.

Both green tea and white tea are healthier to drink than normal tea as they contain antioxidants, which help to tackle cellular deterioration in the body. They also play some role in fighting the early stages of infection (when bacteria are first developing).

And whatever good you have heard about green tea, white tea is better. It has a subtle flavour so if you found green tea a little strong (or grassy) then white tea will help. The only down side is that white tea is more expensive than green tea. Still, for the price of one trip to a coffee shop you can enjoy the world's best tea at home all week. Check out what I believe is the world's finest tea—Jing tea—supplier to some of the world's best restaurants. You can find it at www.jingtea.com.

Support Yourself Whatever Your Decisions

The intention of this section has been to offer you some ideas and suggestions for quickly improving your own diet so you can find what helps you the most. The more you cut out refined sugars, starches, chemicals and industrial processes and replace them with fresh vegetables and fruit, the more you will help your body, strengthen your core and even to lose weight if that interests you. Remember you are aiming for improvement and not perfection. As with all the advice in this book, but especially this chapter—do your own research.

It's so easy to feel guilty or uncertain about anything you eat or drink given the contradictory data. Find a few principles that give you the maximum return for the cost of implementing them, review those choices, and, based on your experience, make better ones in the next time period. So, when you eat junk because you didn't have the resources to eat something more sustaining, remind yourself that your choices are getting better. As you will see in the section on care and support, in the long term, what you eat is less important for your stress levels than your internal emotional state, i.e., what is eating you. We will cover that later in the book.

8c.
Sleep, Rest and Recovery

The benefits of sufficient sleep in turbulent situation are enormous. Many of the negative side effects of stress are massively reduced if you get sufficient sleep to recover. If you wake up tired, then you are much more likely to eat unhealthily and to drink too many stimulants. These stimulants weaken your core and reduce your capacity further as they give your body additional work clearing out the chemicals and caffeine. So what can you do to improve your sleep?

Follow the Research

I know few people who get sufficient sleep. Sleep research offers startling evidence about just how far most of us are from what is best for us. So the first thing to do is figure how many hours you need to maintain and then to strengthen your system. For a few weeks, keep a sleep diary and see how you respond to different amounts of sleep. Also, think of a time when you felt rested. For people in busy jobs and for parents with young children, it can be hard to remember this far back but it's worth a try!

Interestingly, research consistently shows that most people need seven to eight hours of sleep a night to feel rested. I am committed to giving practical advice, so I doubt if that will work for you. I know sleeping five hours a night doesn't work either, but my clients seem keen to keep that up! Further research shows that if you have a sleep deficit (a posh way of saying you're tired) take a nap every four hours. This is often really difficult to do at work. So if you can't increase the hours you have to sleep or nap during the day, improve sleep quality and rest more skilfully during the day.

Follow the USMC/Nursing Example

My colleague and friend in the US, Lt Colonel (Ret) Mike Grice, says this about the USMC's approach to sleep.

Rest and sleep is a cultural thing in the Marine Corps. In combat, it's crucial to conserve energy as you never know how much you will need in the next challenge. We have a saying. "Why stand up when you can sit down, why sit down when you can lie down, why be awake when you can be asleep?"

During my last tour in Afghanistan, I had to brief very senior officers and political leaders from the multi-national force. It was common for half these people to be asleep as I set up my presentation. They had created a precious 15 minutes of down time so they made the most of it. I knew that as soon as I was ready to start, they would sit up and participate.

It's not uncommon waiting in a helicopter pick-up zone to see half of the people who are waiting to be asleep on the ground. I've actually slept in the back of a helicopter on the way into a mission because I knew I had an hour before we hit the landing zone. What else are you going to do? And when would I get the chance again?

You can develop the ability to power down and then quickly power back up. I can sleep for 15 minutes and wake up ready and refreshed. Why? Because I have trained myself to do it and it is part of Marines culture.

You may not be able to do this in your work, but within the rhythm of your day and week, there are going to be times when some team members are busy and others are not. You can allow individuals to rest within that rhythm. Maybe you can go somewhere and you can power down for 30 minutes. You don't necessarily have to lie down and go to sleep, but the lessons we've learned through our training and also through a lifetime study is that short rest periods maximize your energy conservation.

Being able to take a few minutes to close your eyes, clear your mind, and come back refreshed is very, very beneficial. But it's a cultural thing. And it starts from an acceptance that if you want to deliver excellence, you put the mission first and do whatever you need to perform that mission. And working 18 hours a day and pretending you're not tired because of some foolish macho culture is not putting the mission first. So if you don't take advantage of those micro opportunities to recuperate, then you will be fruitlessly expending your energy and expending it badly. Take a few minutes, come back stronger.[62]

A friend who helped with proofing this book told me that his mother had learnt the same wisdom when studying to become a nurse in England in the 1950s. So deeply was the principle ingrained that she followed the instruction until her death at the age of 80, and insisted that family members should do the same!

I don't have the skill to sleep whenever I want, but I do rest whenever I can, even if it's for a few breaths (literally). It just breaks the momentum of slipping down the back of the stress curve. So take micro-breaks and promote a mission first approach instead of an appearance first approach. And if you are a leader, and can influence group norms, engage your people on the performance aspect of this.

The Research on Working All Night

Clients involved with intense projects or deals often work all night. My advice here is to follow the science, which says:

1. Don't work all night! There is too much cognitive impairment for it to be worth the effort (about a 40% drop in cognitive ability).
2. If you must work all night, take a two hour break around 1am-3am. This is typically the best time in your daily energy cycle to take one sleep cycle (which usually lasts around 2-2.5 hours.
3. If you can't do that, then introduce a routine of rest for 20 minutes every 4 hours, and set up a room with camp beds.   If the task is important enough to warrant all night working, follow the research and do it properly.

Create a Sleep Ritual

Sometimes, you won't be able to get the quantity of sleep you need so improve the quality. The key to this is to create a sleep ritual.

Simply, this is a process that helps you to maximise your chances of restful sleep, however long. As with nearly everything there are influencing factors that maximise the chances of getting quality sleep. Find a routine that works and then follow it as much as you can. So think about when you have slept most restfully and think about what happened in the day or hours before you went to sleep. Consciously apply some of the things that happened fortuitously. Here are some suggestions from my research and client experience.

1. Minimise stimulant intake (caffeinated drinks or energy drinks) throughout the day and take no more stimulants after noon unless it's essential. As we all know, caffeine makes you feel edgy, but it can also weaken your bladder wall temporarily, so you will have to go to the toilet more often and when you don't really need to. If you drink lots of coffee and you have had to get up in the middle of the night to go to the toilet and have hardly any urine come out, cut the caffeine. You

will sleep more peacefully as you won't have to get up to go to the toilet.

2.   If you eat junk food, eat it earlier in the day and eat healthier foods and smaller meals as the day progresses. This minimises your body's workload and reduces the chance of disturbances caused by digestion. Also, reduce alcohol to one glass of wine a night.

3.   On stressful days, work hard to use up the chemicals before entering a calming period. I speak about this in the movement section so I won't repeat it here.

4.   Get any potentially activating thoughts out of your head. When finishing work for the day, write down anything going round your head. This could be reflections about what has happened or what needs to happen tomorrow. Do the same at home for personal matters (and persistent work issues) before the last 45 minutes of your day. Keep the list handy, because you may have other things to add to the list as you relax further.   Then as the thoughts return, remind yourself that they are already on the list and so you can let them go.

5.   . Our spaces have become contaminated. That is, our home space is also used for work. This is may be unavoidable but the more you can have your bedroom or sleep space just for sleep, the better. If you are working away, clear anything that reminds you of work from your sleep space before you go into slow down. This will take five to 10 minutes, but you quickly get into the habit of working in a tidier manner and it's worth the investment for the clarity it brings

6.   Try a warm bath to help you to relax (hot baths tend to activate unless you can do it early enough). Epsom salts can improve this further. Keep topping up the bath if you get cold.

7. Meditate or Pray. If you do pray, then I can recommend the benefits of morning and evening prayer as a way to add structure, focus and support to your day. If your religious beliefs prelude prayer I would encourage you take up some form of meditation. There is nothing esoteric of complicated about the type of meditation I am suggesting here. It is simply a brief time where you sit quietly and allow you mind to become clear. One thing you can also combine this with is to express appreciation or gratitude for all the good things in your life, large and small. I find writing these in a journal increases the power of this activity. It also generates coherent heart rhythms. I will be focusing on this more in the Care and Support section so read more there.

8. Stimulate natural melatonin production. Melatonin is a hormone produced by your body that regulates the sleep-wake cycle. To activate it, go into slow down mode and eliminate bright lights during the final 30 to 45 minutes of your evening. So turn off the TV and read with a reading light. Deliberately move slowly too. Perform a relaxation exercise that suits you. I am a big fan of the *Autogenic* method as you can use it for normal stress situations but there are lots of apps available.

9. Read fiction. I like to read before going to bed. I only read fiction as non-fiction generates too much thinking. A possible exception is reading boring non-fiction. Mike Grice, the retired Marine I mentioned, recommends his book, *On Gunnery: The Art and Science of Field Artillery*. It's technically non-fiction but you'll find it hard to read more than five pages without falling to sleep!

On a scientific note, as you want to give yourself no further stimulation as you approach bed time, reading a boring non-fiction book may help. You can also read it in a way that tires your eyes by decreasing the angle between your eyes and the page. Simply, read lying down instead of sitting up and hold the book as flat to your chest as you can and still be able to read it. This makes it harder to read, tires the eyes and makes you more likely to fall asleep as you are already in the correct position.

10. If you still have trouble sleeping, consider using a natural supplement, such as melatonin, vitamin B6, or chelated magnesium.

More Rest, Faster Recovery

I have just covered some suggestions for improving the quality of your sleep. I would now like to share some ideas of increasing and improving the rest you get during the day. This reduces the sleep or energy deficit you have because you'll use less energy and you'll stay more relaxed throughout the day. Better rest can also improve the quality of your sleep as you as able to switch off more completely.

Take Breaks When You Are at Your Best

It is not helpful for you to remain at your desk for long periods as it is impossible to maintain the quality of your thinking. This deterioration can go unnoticed if you don't stop to review the quality of your work. If you take a few weeks to actually notice the quality of your thinking–when you are at your best, how long it takes to get into that thinking, maintain it, and then drop off–you can maximise the return on the times when you are at your best as you can reserve those times for doing your most important work.

As your concentration starts to drop off, take short breaks throughout the day. Regard 90 minutes as a maximum for staying on one thing because it is the outside level of our powers of concentration. The actual optimum could be 45 to 50 minutes, but it all depends on what you are actually doing. You can prolong your ability to concentrate by varying the tasks you do. Take enough time to give something quality time and, when you sense the quality dropping, look to make a change to a different activity and then move back to the original work.

Control Your Position on the Curve

We are now going to look at fast ways to quickly regain focus and to stop the momentum of a challenging situation pushing you to the left-hand side of the four quadrant model.

To change the negative momentum of a situation in which you find yourself, you first need to be able to sense where the momentum is pulling you. The sooner you can detect a potential shift in momentum as the effects of stress become negative, the faster you will be able to get things back to where you want them to be. To go back to the chronic stress curves as shown by Swank and Marchand from World War II, you want to be noticing the shift as close to top of the curve as you can while minimising the period of over-confidence.

If you would like to improve your anticipatory skills further, review your stress curve work and be sure to read the chapter on brain control. In the meantime, what things can we do to change the momentum and to recover from stressful situations more quickly?

Noticing and accepting where you are is the first thing to do. It may be disappointing to face reality, but it's necessary and inevitable. It's important to remember that self-awareness and acceptance are part of performing at a high level. So get clear on your peaks—what they look, feel, and sound like. To be at your best, you need to accept that falling off the peak and working to get back on is a key skill to develop.

If you catch the shift in momentum early, you want to do something that will help to stimulate the positive emotions on the right-hand side of the four quadrant model straight away. So the next focus is:

Do The Things That Take You to the Right Quadrants

Think of all the things that help you generate emotions such as appreciation, gratitude, engagement, openness, receptivity. Make a list of all the things you can think of that could help you do this.

Consider things you can do in:

- One to five minutes
- 10 to 15 minutes
- 30 minutes or more

Then do those activities throughout the day. Here's a list of things my clients have found helpful.

One to Five Minute Recoveries

Breathe deeply. Make fun of the challenge. Talk with colleagues about stressors. Call a friend. Have a distraction to help regain focus, e.g. listen to music, watch funny videos on the Internet, read an article. Focus on the good/exciting thing about the event. Smile. Read an inspirational quote and have a minute's reflection on it. Then think about how it relates to your current work. Review my picture of what amazing looks like. Drink water and remember to eat. Move and stretch.

10 to 15 minutes

Reward myself with little things on a regular basis. Agree on priorities with colleagues to increase alignment. Meditate. Have defined detachment periods. Turn off my computer and write out a plan. Pause, breathe, then write the first 15 minutes of actions down and then take a break. Have 10 minutes on the Web. Take a walk. Take a step back–think about why I am doing what I am doing. Refocus on the big picture. Talk to someone with a different perspective.

30 minutes +

Eat lunch with co-workers. Go for a long run. Go to a yoga class. Take a nap. Move to a new work environment. Find some way or somewhere to have quiet for tough thinking tasks (e.g., wear earplugs, noise cancelling headphones, work in a separate room, or from home). Converse with someone outside the situation. Go to bed and wake up early to continue working. Break the stressors into more manageable, actionable chunks. Exercise outside. Spend time with people you love. Have a beer.

It's helpful when thinking about what you can do to remember the importance of feeling that you are winning or making progress in something you find meaningful. For example, if I need to reset my emotional state, I sometimes work in my garden. The movement helps use the hormones and I find the progress I see rewarding.

When you know your own preferences you can structure these breaks into what you do. And prepare ahead of time (e.g., save articles to read, set up play lists for generating different emotions, etc.) That way you can go straight to the redirection instead of wondering what to do. This always has the effect of reducing the time it takes to complete the momentum shift.

And remember, the fastest way to recover is to avoid having to recover at all!

Turn Everything Off Every Week

One thing that massively aids recovery is if you can turn everything off at least once a week (for a whole day if possible). When we become over-stimulated, we tend to demand stimulation everywhere. So we listen to pop music instead of calmer forms of music (or even silence) and eat faster, more stimulating food. We check our phones obsessively and are always checking in. Once you are able to get ahead of the crises, I encourage you to turn off the phone, and have a quiet day doing as little as you can stand. Do no exciting activities, just ones that generate openness and moderate interest. Relax.

If you work in a PSF then I can imagine how hard it may be for people to accept that you will be unavailable. So you may need to have a one to two month focus on "necessary communication" before turning off the phone. I know people who have bought what they describe as a "*bat phone*" after the superhero, Batman. Only one or two people have that number and it is only ever used for work if there is an emergency that Batman would respond to. Your job maybe to tackle other peoples crises, you don't have to live your life in crisis mode.

Read Anticancer: A New Way of Life

One of the most influential books I have read with scientifically proven ways to improve your PNS and overall well-being was the fantastic *Anticancer: A New Way of Life,* by Dr David Servan-Schreiber. The author was a psychiatrist who fought cancer in his early 30s and couldn't understand why no one had any advice for how he could change his life style to minimise the chances of his cancer returning. So he did his own research and gathered together everything that has been shown to help push you along the survival bell curve. The result is perhaps the best book on overall well-being I have ever read. Dr Servan-Schreiber applied many of the principles himself and managed to extend his life by nearly 20 years before the cancer returned. He passed away in 2011 after writing his final piece of inspiration, *not the last goodbye*. I whole-heartedly recommend all his work.

Summary

- Strengthening your core, or PNS, helps you to attract and accumulate resources to help you tackle the challenges you face.
- This starts with improving your breathing and also involves movement and exercise, food and drink, and healthy sleep and recovery.
- Aim to use the hormones your body has produced that day by moving more frequently and energetically.
- Instead of "*Work hard, play hard,*" try "*work hard, play easy.*" Exercise gently to build core fitness before doing more strenuous activity.
- Our modern diet based on processed food, refined sugars and starches, and chemicals suits no one. Work to reduce them all substituting them with food as close to its natural state as possible.
- Your body doesn't crave junk food when stressed. It craves naturally produced food with high energy content which tends to be sugary and fatty (it craves salty food for the minerals). Again simply substitute sugary, salty and fatty junk food for natural sources (or better quality junk!)
- When you can't be good, simply be less bad and do what you can to aid your recovery when you do have the resources.
- Drink enough liquid so your body can remain hydrated as it cleans out your system.

- Green tea and White tea have been shown to aid your body in its restorative activities. Drink those as you cut down on caffeine.
- Most of us need seven to eight hours of sleep a night to be fully rested. This can be difficult so concentrate first on improving the quality of what sleep you do get and take a nap during the day if at all possible.
- Create a sleep ritual to help your mind and body prepare for sleep and follow it as much as you can.
- Take short periods of rest and recovery every 90 minutes.
- Recovery time could simply be distracting activities. Where possible though find something that requires movement and but gives you a sense of progress (e.g. gardening).

9.
Brain Function: John Boyd and Maneuver Warfare – Your Unlikely Stress Teachers

"Battles are won by slaughter and maneuver. The greater the general, the more he contributes in maneuver, the less he demands in slaughter." [63]

Winston Churchill

I will be focusing on ways to improve brain function in the next two chapters. I want to look at something called maneuver warfare and the work of philosopher, John Boyd. Both have interesting things to say about how to keep our thinking clear, reduce conflict in turbulent situations, and minimise damage.

Could We Learn from Extreme Situations?

Using military strategy in the civilian world may seem like a strange idea, but I think you will see that it can be used to understand and dissolve/resolve mismatches between you and your environment. Integrating principles from Boyd (and other philosophers) can transform your approach to stress and help you live more successfully. And this body of wisdom integrates beautifully with the latest theories on entrepreneurship, innovation and strategy.

Since getting to know Boyd's ideas after stumbling over him in Tom Peters' *Reimagine*, I am much more able to appreciate intuitively a fast moving situation and quickly figure out how to influence. The principles of maneuver warfare (which I will briefly explain) are applicable to a nation, a company, and to an individual. So what is it and how does it differ from more conventional approaches to resolving conflict or mismatches with our environment?

Maneuver Warfare vs. Attritional Warfare

Maneuver warfare has been around for as long as there has been conflict. The most famous treatise on it is *The Sun Tzu* or *Art of War,* which was written about 2,300 years ago in China.

Briefly, there are two key types of conflict on a grand scale—attritional conflict and maneuver conflict. Both are designed to eliminate "the fight" of our opponent. Attritional conflict seeks to do this by removing the opponent's **ability** to fight. The maneuverist approach seeks to remove the opponent's **desire** or will to fight.

Attritional Conflict

Attritional conflict, or slaughter as Churchill described it, is what most of us would regard as conventional warfare. The focus is on such things as military firepower with the destruction of the adversary and their ability to wage war as the measure of success.

This approach works best when the situation is stable and the relationships among the key elements are understood with a clear causal chain (one thing leads to another). Any change in the situation is controlled or, if it can't be controlled, it is managed. One may wish to engage in this form of battle when you have vastly superior resources than your opponent and an ability and/or willingness to sustain whatever casualties you need to cause the destruction or surrender of the enemy.

Maneuver Warfare

A maneuverist approach to warfare emphasizes innovation, flexibility, and responsiveness. Troops are given the freedom to seize fleeting opportunities and to respond creatively and collaboratively to events. Any change in the initial conditions is a threat to the plans in a conventional approach to battle. With the maneuverist approach, such a change is seen as a potential opportunity and often will be supported to speed up and magnify its effects—just as an entrepreneur thinks about a dynamic marketplace.

Instead of defeating the enemy through destruction of their resources, you remove their will to fight. This can be done by making the environment so chaotic or terrifying that the enemy loses all will or courage to fight. The US Marine Corps " *Warfighting*" manual says:

"[Maneuver warfare] *seeks to shatter the enemy's cohesion through a variety of rapid, focused, and unexpected actions which create a turbulent and rapidly deteriorating situation with which the enemy cannot cope.*"

In terms of the stress response, this is an attempt to cause not fight-flight but freeze.

David, the First Maneuverist?

A great example of maneuverist principles comes from Bible. David fought the superior foe, Goliath, and destroyed the Philistines' will to fight. The giant had been causing terror in Israel's ranks through daily taunts and was destroying their courage (their will to fight). No one would fight him so David volunteered. Refusing the King's armour, he relied on speed and surprise to disable his superior opponent (with his sling). He used Goliath's own weapons against him to finish the job. The Bible says this prompted a stunning battle field reversal, broke the will of the Philistines, and saved Israel.

Win Without Fighting

Most interestingly for us, a maneuverist approach can be used to create a future that encompasses both positions which dissolves the reason for your opponent to fight. The general is able *"to win without fighting"* as it says in the *Art of War.*[64]

For example, when Napoleon returned to Paris from exile, his old troops were sent to defeat his much smaller revolutionary force. Napoleon rejected battle and approached the "enemy" army alone. Unarmed, he persuaded them to join him. Few people record this as a great battle but it's one of his greatest maneuvers–a total victory with no loss of life on either side. This is the highest level of skill a general can show. Use of violence nearly always creates a greater mismatch in our environment (even if it sometimes unavoidable).

In business, technological innovation resonates with maneuverist principles. Instead of engaging an incumbent market leader directly on their terms, you create a product using ideas from another field to eliminate their advantage–think of Apple and their development of iTunes. iTunes transformed the music and mobile phone industries from one dominated by hardware to one dominated by software and apps. They have changed the way business is run in their markets.

Organisational Constraints

Given the benefits of maneuverist principles, you may wonder why anyone would fight any other way. The reason is simple–organisational constraints. It is all very well wanting your people to be adaptive, dynamic, fluid, and innovative. To foster that, however, you need to create an organisation built on shared perspective, trust, and collaboration. This takes a great deal of time (sometimes time we don't have). This type of environment goes counter to the strong urge most leaders have to control things especially when under stress. Few of us can resist the temptation to interfere when we have the resources.

A leader of maneuverist forces is, "*In command, and out of control*," to quote US Marine Corps Lt. General Paul Van Riper,[65] one of the finest exponents of a maneuverist approach in recent times.

Different Situations, Different Approaches

It is usually most helpful to rely on the maneuverist's assets of adaptability, fluidity and tempo to protect yourself and to get ahead of what is happening if you can. Any major battle usually involves combinations of both–grinding down the enemy and also seeking to hasten this process by deception, surprise or maneuver. The important thing is to be sure you are applying the most suitable approach for your environment and not simply because that is your preference.

However, to be successful in any conflict, you have to be willing and able to engage in both types of conflict. It may be that someone we have to work with doesn't want to work collaboratively and so some (non-physical) conflict will be unavoidable. Engaging in direct action is most profitable when you can break your challenge into small parts that you can isolate. Then you can apply sufficient resources to overwhelm the task. This makes a difficult task easy.

We are now going to briefly look at John Boyd's work. This will deepen our understanding of how his work can transform not only your understanding of stress, but also your ability to deal with it. Whilst Boyd is most famous for his contributions to maneuver warfare, our main interest is in his ideas on how to win in relatively peaceful or non–military environments.

John Boyd's Contribution

Whilst John Boyd is not the originator of maneuverist strategy, he was a moderniser of it and helped to reinvigorate the USA's approach to warfighting.[66] He is most famous for his decision-action process called the OODA loop (pronounced uu-da) [covered in the next chapter].

Boyd began his military career as a pilot in the US Air Force. He was so good he earned the nickname "*40 Second Boyd*" for his ability beat other pilots in combat within 40 seconds. He literally wrote the (first) book on air-to-air combat, *Aerial Attack Study*. His work with planes reached a philosophical peak with something called energy maneuverability which explained why one plane was superior to another and how that advantage could be used or countered.[67] EM Theory is now one of the main theoretical tools for designing new fighter jets. [There's more on this on the website].

The Patterns of Winning and Losing?

Whilst working at the Pentagon, Boyd became interested in other forms of conflict and he focused on land based conflict. His work helped to articulate ideas that had been fermenting in the US Marine Corps and they used his ideas to help rewrite their battle doctrine (This is *Warfighting*, a document I have already quoted).

He continued this progression to more general forms of interaction in retirement when he combined fields such as philosophy, learning, physics, math, biology, and religion. Boyd's later work is focused on building harmonious relationships with any anything or anyone that could interfere with your ability to act freely and independently in pursuit of your goals. It puts physical conflict in the right place – as the last resort.

Conflict emerges when there has been a failure to learn by one party or the other (or both) in how to reduce this mismatch between them and their surrounding environment. This mismatch is then expensively "resolved" through escalating conflict. In such situations, you want to be fast, lethal, sneaky and unpredictable. But you only fight when there are no other options.

When you move beyond his earlier military connections you can see his entire body of work as an attempt to answer one question:

What are the fundamental patterns of winning and losing?

Boyd showed that no system can be fully understood without involving other neighbouring systems. Therefore, to be successful in your chosen domain (for any duration) you have to cultivate an intimate understanding and appreciation of your surroundings and the entities or agents within it. And then you must appreciate how your chosen field influences, and is influenced by, surrounding domains or environments. This means that indirect action, in complex situations, is likely to generate superior results to direct, head on action because it tends to maintain the web of relationships between the neighbouring systems. You also need to explore how time could help or hinder your efforts.

How to Stress Someone Out

Isolation and interaction was a consistent focus for Boyd. Success demands that you combine them as you understand and then shape your environment. We lose when we become too isolated. Winning requires high levels of interaction within your environment which maintains and strengthens key relationships.

To explore isolation and interaction and how it links to stress, I am going to take a close look at a summary passage in one of Boyd's later presentations, *"The Strategic Game of ? and ?"* (The missing words become *Isolation and Interaction*). This passage showed me that he understood stress in a way that few other experts have before or since. I thought he must have been studying my thought processes as I suffered my burn out.

Below is Boyd's description of how he wanted the losing commander to think and act in a conflict situation.[68] Read the passage and then I will explain what I took from it.

To defeat someone you need to:

Probe and test the adversary and any allies that may rally to his side, to unmask strengths, weaknesses, maneuvers, and intentions:

Exploit critical differences of opinion, internal contradictions, frictions, obsessions, etc., to ferment mistrust, sow discord, and shape both the adversary's and allies' perceptions of the world. This in turn will:

Create an atmosphere of mental confusion, contradiction of feeling, indecisiveness and panic

Manipulate or undermine the adversary's plans and actions

Make it difficult if not impossible for allies to aid the adversary during his time of trial

They experience...

Various combinations of uncertainty, doubt, confusion, self-deception, indecision, fear, panic, discouragement, despair, etc.

Overall Message

The ability to operate at a faster tempo or rhythm than an adversary enables one to fold the adversary back inside himself so that he can neither appreciate nor keep-up with what's going on. He will become disoriented or confused;

Unless such menacing pressure is relieved, adversary will experience various combinations of uncertainty, doubt, confusion, self-deception, indecision, fear, panic, discouragement, despair, etc., which will further:

Disorient or twist his mental images/impressions of what's happening;

Thereby

Disrupt his mental/physical maneuvers for dealing with such a menace;

Thereby

Overload his mental/physical capacity to adapt or endure;

Thereby

Collapse his ability to carry on.

(© Col. John R. Boyd estate)

If You Can Create It, You Can Stop It

This passage led to one of the few genuine epiphanies of my professional life. I realised that if someone could cause a breakdown in mental, physical, and moral functioning, you could prevent it. The steps of my break down, whilst chaotic and bewildering at the time, were actually predictable. I realized I could use these Boydian insights to work out how close someone is to breaking and then help them find the fastest way to recover.

The most frightening aspect though was the realisation that I had unconsciously done to myself what a skilled enemy would have tried to do had they wanted to defeat me. Both metaphorically and literally, I had been my own worst enemy. And when I begin working with clients who already in deep trouble, they are doing the exact same things.

How Boyd's Work Links Back to Ours

The above passage may seem to have little relevance to a non-military situation at first glance. The conflict we face is nearly always with our environment and not with someone who is out to get us. I would argue that conflict is conflict and all forms of conflict relate to how you interact with or become isolated from your environment.

Any superior military leader will use the environment to hasten an opponent's demise. So we could reasonably say that as people are part of the environment in which we operate, it's the environment that becomes so chaotic and dangerous that it causes someone to give up. And a general's goal is not to defeat an enemy force per se but to create a more harmonious relationship with his or her environment. That his or her focus is on enemy forces is simply because that is the fastest moving and most threatening aspect of the immediate environment. If we accept this assertion, we can conclude that all conflict is a conflict with our environment. Whether we use hugs, words, bullets or bombs to resolve the conflict comes down to how far the mismatch with our environment has progressed.

This broader, most holistic perspective reduces the chance of our becoming fixated on one apparent obstacle (or opponent) with our environment. Instead we focus on our relationship with our environment, of which the obstacle is a part to be considered as we shape and create our own future.

So read it again with my notes attached on how this relates to stress in dynamic situations.

Probe and test the adversary and any allies that may rally to his side, to unmask strengths, weaknesses, maneuvers, and intentions.

Challenging situations ask fundamental questions and expose hidden weaknesses. A deteriorating situation rarely gives you opportunity to use your strengths. If it did, you would probably be able to move at the required speed. It is important to know yourself, especially your strengths and weaknesses and how you react in difficult situations. This will help you predict how much trouble you are going to have if you have to use your weaknesses. This is why we have focused so much on preparation, and mastery.

Notice also the importance he places on alliances. The Sun Tzu also says strategy and alliances are the first too things the wise general should focus on if he wishes to be victorious.

Exploit critical differences of opinion, internal contradictions, frictions, obsessions, etc., to ferment mistrust, sow discord, and shape both the adversary's and allies' perceptions of the world.

Internal coherence and trust are crucial. Trusting yourself is essential as self-doubt causes you to focus internally and will cause you to fall behind emerging events. A loss of trust in a team draws the focus of attention inside the team instead of keeping it external— the source of the real danger. The team members' perceptions are now being shaped by their emotions and reactions to events instead of the reality of the situation. Everyone begins to wonder if they should be protecting themselves against their colleagues. This matches well with Porges' work on creating a safe social environment.

This in turn will:

Create an atmosphere of mental confusion, contradiction of feeling, indecisiveness and panic.

When you become stressed, fear and anxiety combine to turn everything into a threat. It looks as if there are problems (and potential attacks) everywhere. Relaxation and recovery is impossible. Your emotional swings become much more volatile as your whole physiology is out of balance. It feels like you are on a roller coaster just sitting at your desk. Also, commitment and desire are crucial factors in maintaining your willingness to pay the price of your perseverance.

Manipulate or undermine the adversary's plans and actions.

Because of this inability to focus, any constructive efforts to improve things are quickly stopped as we begin to do something else (we are trying to stamp out fires everywhere). You then stop that and start another thing. Ultimately you achieve nothing and put no fires out. This leads you to question your basic understanding of the situation. We are looking for some sense of safety and stability either in the social environment or in our strategy -the expression of how we understand our situation. This is deeply threatening and causes you to pause and lose momentum–a dangerous thing in a fast moving situation.

Make it difficult if not impossible for allies to aid the adversary during his time of trial.

This is a fascinating aspect of turbulent situations. We can't tackle them alone but the stress makes us far less likely to ask for help. The quality of someone's allies (a.k.a friends) is one of the best single measures of their likelihood to get through a turbulent period

They experience...

Various combinations of uncertainty, doubt, confusion, self-deception, indecision, fear, panic, discouragement, despair, etc.

You oscillate between anger and despair depending on how dangerous you perceive the situation to be. Eventually, you collapse from exhaustion. Your "*vehicle*"–in this case, your body–has broken down from the excessive acceleration and braking with no recuperation.

Overall Message

The ability to operate at a faster tempo or rhythm than an adversary enables one to fold the adversary back inside himself so that he can neither appreciate nor keep-up with what's going on. He will become disoriented or confused;

Falling behind an emerging situation leaves you with more and more to do with less and less time to do it. This impairs and delays communication and reduces the quality of subsequent intelligence. This is why it is so important to anticipate and prepare for a challenge as that is how you manage to keep up with the situation. We will consider the impact of speed and tempo shortly as it is often misunderstood.

Unless such menacing pressure is relieved, the adversary will experience various combinations of uncertainty, doubt, confusion, self-deception, indecision, fear, discouragement, panic, despair, etc., which will further:

Disorient or twist his mental images/impressions of what's happening;

Look at all the emotions from the left hand, incoherent quadrants from chapter 6! Stress hormones will be flooding your brain (especially the neo–cortex) at this point making clear thinking impossible. This causes viral stupidity. You lose the ability to sensibly assess risk, in part, because you cannot access your memory (crucial for threat assessment), and so to play it safe your brain assumes that everything is life threatening. You will either freeze and stop taking any risks or begin taking extremely dangerous risks because you are no longer thinking.

Thereby...

Disrupt his mental/physical maneuvers for dealing with such a menace;

If everything is a threat you can't really defend yourself. Increasingly, your actions become irrational as you fight threats that are not even there. Also, you will be so far behind events that things will have changed before you can execute whatever you were planning to do.

Thereby...

Overload his mental/physical capacity to adapt or endure;

Being stressed all the time leaves you physically and mentally drained. Stress hormones cause emotional flooding, which then leads to nightmare fantasies and deep pessimism about your chances of winning or changing anything. As a result, you stop trying and become powerless. You may have had the skill to tackle the threat but you no longer have the motivation and willingness to do what it takes. And you will have already cut yourself off from external relations, so the ties that could have helped or prompted action don't motivate either.

Thereby...

Collapse his ability to carry on.

Game over. We can put a fork in you now because you're done. I certainly was.

We Do All This to Ourselves

In this passage, Boyd was talking about doing all this to an opponent. I didn't need an "opponent" and nor do you. The mismatch with your environment is what you are "*opposing*". Your stress response, a lack of awareness, and living in a hostile environment will do it all for you. Failure is nearly always an inside job. This is why you need to protect and improve your thought processes and improve your environmental interaction and connection. If you can keep your thinking clear, you will have the best chance of thriving in a difficult situation. That will be the topic of the next chapter.

Churchill Revisited

Let's go back to the quotation from Churchill at the start of this chapter. Here is the full version from his book, *The World Crisis:*

> *Battles are won by slaughter and manoeuvre. The greater the general, the more he contributes in manoeuvre, the less he demands in slaughter. The theory which has exalted the 'bataille d'usure' or 'battle of*

wearing down' into a foremost position, is contradicted by history and would be repulsed by the greatest captains of the past. Nearly all the battles which are regarded as masterpieces of the military art, from which have been derived the foundation of states and the fame of commanders, have been battles of manoeuvre in which very often the enemy has found himself defeated by some novel expedient or device, some queer, swift, unexpected thrust or stratagem. In many such battles the losses of the victors have been small.

As Churchill says above, the maneuverist approach to dealing with challenges and conflict within our environment minimizes resource usage and maximizes impact. It's a focus on resourcefulness rather than just resources.

The thinking pioneered by Boyd and his intellectual ancestors is something that takes time to develop. However, cultivating the ability to refuse the apparently inevitable direct conflict and to find a way to move around it (through adjacent systems), transforms your ability to understand and successfully navigate turbulent situations. At its simplest level, it is learning to dance more skilfully between isolation and integration, of ensuring that whatever you do to understand the parts, you always integrate that picture into a broader whole.

The challenge for you is to increase your personal capacity for adaptability, creativity, flexibility, your morale and the strength of your relationships with those around you. These capabilities will allow you to feel comfortable with being uncomfortable in a fast moving situation. This will mean that you won't need to "*control*" the situation as you will be in control of yourself and your response to turbulence.

In this chapter, I have demonstrated how reapplying maneuverist principles to your life can help you deal with stress more effectively and give you a better chance of avoiding stressful situations all together. What are the key points for you to focus on?

Summary

- There are two main approaches to resolving conflict, removing someone's ability to fight (attritional) or removing their desire or will to fight (maneuver).
- Maneuver relies less on resources as it does on resourcefulness. It utilises such qualities as adaptability, fluidity and unpredictability.
- It is possible to reverse the approach John Boyd took to stressing out an opponent to strengthen your ability to deal with stressful situations.
- We can also use Boyd's later work that focused much more on how to win/learn in any (peaceful) environment.
- Instead of seeing the environment as something to defeat or something that is trying to defeat you, focus on removing the need or desire for conflict by increasing the harmony between you and what is happening in your environment.
- To do this find ways to use your strengths, neutralise your weaknesses, and strengthen alliances with others.
- Alliances and harmony reduce discord and build trust which creates a safe social environment.
- This allows you to focus externally on dissolving the friction and increasing your tempo so that you can get ahead of the situation and begin to shape events.
- Time, and its corollary, speed, are crucial. However, it is not absolute speed that counts but the relative speed between you and your environment/ opponent (if appropriate). When deciding what to do, consider the impact it would have on your speed (will it

increase your dynamism?) and on the impact it has on the situation (will it slow it down/shift the momentum in your desired direction?)

- The clearer you can be with your aims (and plans) the easier it is to build alignment with your allies. Clarity of aims and alignment are more important than any actual plans.

- As your strategy matches your environment more and more closely (and as your learning increases) you will be able to predict and anticipate what is going to happen next. This gives you confidence and encourages further decisive action.

10.
Building Immunity to Viral Stupidity

In this chapter, we will look at how your thinking can become distorted in stressful situations or, as I was saying earlier, how you can catch viral stupidity. I will use John Boyd's most famous idea–the Observe-Orient-Decide-Act Loop, known as the OODA (uuda) loop–as a framework for this dialogue. One of the themes of this book (and Boyd's work) is the importance of the right type of interaction and temporary isolation from your environment. Clear thinking is crucial to maintaining the most helpful dance of interaction and isolation. Isolation, unless it is used to increase future capacity, is nearly always damaging in dynamic situations because the mismatch between you and your environment nearly always builds during your isolation.

So, in this chapter we'll be considering:
- What's the difference between average "thinking" and you thinking at your best?
- What causes you (or anyone) to catch viral stupidity?
- What can you do about it?

How We "Think" Normally
The popular way of drawing Boyd's OODA loop shows it to be a simple thought-action process. We first observe what is happening. From the information we collect, we then orient, that is, understand or appreciate what is happening. This leads us to a decision, which we

then execute. Completion of the action takes us back to the beginning and we start again.

I have put "think" in quotation marks in the heading as there isn't actually that much thinking in this cycle. The observation and orientation are more to confirm previous understanding than to make a new assessment. The brain looks for signals in the environment that match previous experiences. We find a pattern that worked well enough in the past and we repeat that.

Figure 11.The Popular OODA Diagram

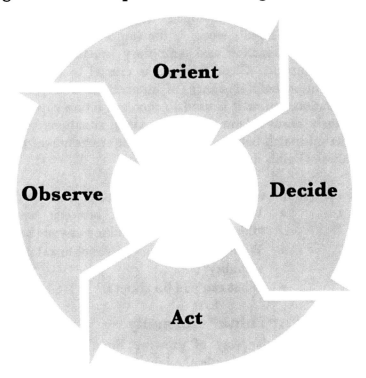

Pattern recognition is a critical part of successfully navigating challenging situations. The problems come from choosing too quickly or failing to notice differences between the last time it worked and what is happening today. Checking quickly to confirm the situation is the same as last time leaves us vulnerable in changing situations. This is because things can look as if they are similar to what has happened before and then evolve into something else. Unfortunately, our assumption that this is like last time can lead us to dismiss as noise, the sometimes subtle but crucial differences. Given the well–known flaw in this approach, why do we do it? Because it's an efficient use of our energy and thinking power most of time.

Making the Most of Our Limited Capacity

It's important to minimize inessential thought because, despite the amazing size and power of the brains, far less is available for conscious thought than was previously imagined. To get around this, the brain looks to make automatic (or unconscious) as many thoughts and actions as possible. This approach makes more of our limited conscious thinking power available for non-standard activities that resist mental automation.

If the unconscious processing is known and periodically reviewed to ensure relevance, this will make us better. In fact automatic processing is the essence of learning and the cultivation of mastery, something we looked at with the paratroopers. However, such thinking can give us lots of trouble when we have untested, unconscious thoughts and emotions. Both distort our decision making process especially when we are in novel situations.

The Elephant and the Rider

One historic metaphor for the recent neurological findings in just how much of our thinking is unconscious comes from The Buddha. He compared the brain to a huge elephant with a rider perched on top. The elephant represents the automatic part of the brain and the rider the conscious part. In theory, we could describe the rider as the *leader* but he or she gets to lead only where the elephant wants to go and only if the elephant trusts the rider's guidance. Therefore, our ability to guide our elephant is based on influence rather than on power. Influence with such a powerful force depends on the quality of our long term-relationship rather than what we do in the moment.

When the elephant become stressed, the rider's influence drops further, and the elephant can run out of control. When I first heard this metaphor, I recalled the last time I had become stressed or angry, and it certainly resonated as to how it felt. I didn't feel in control of what I was doing as my emotions were in charge.

On the other side, this metaphor offers a positive image of just how much power is available if you improve your relationship between conscious and unconscious thinking. This is done best during calm situations. Thorough preparation and anticipation give us the best chance of thinking and behaving as we would like in challenging situations when the elephant becomes nervous or agitated and needs to be calmed.

Another reason why anticipation is important is that you can prepare your whole self (mind and body) for the challenge. Life-like practice can have the same effect on the brain as actually doing something. Saying you'll be fine is not the same as knowing you'll be fine because of all the preparation you have done. As you tackle challenging situation you need to be mindful of the kinds of things that irritate your elephant. Most of us usually have triggers that can cause a strong emotional reaction. It's helpful to appreciate what these are and then take steps to disconnect or harness any unhelpful responses.

What's Wrong with the Popular OODA?

There is something potentially amiss with the popular OODA loop. If taken out of context (seen as an end in itself) we can forget that the fundamental cause of stress—a mismatch between us and our environment–is often caused by weak or unhelpful connections to our environment.

Initially, this loss of connection with the environment may go unnoticed or be dismissed as undeserving of your attention [think about what the politicians and bankers were saying at the start of the financial crash]. It is only when the friction reaches a high enough level and results deteriorate that you have to respond. Typically, you do more of what you were doing as we try to accommodate the change because you have no new information to suggest that a bigger change would be more helpful than more of the same.

To act successfully you must cultivate deeper connections with your environment. This diagram shows no external interaction. Isolation can and will increase the mismatch and friction. The two exceptions to this are when we are in a situation that is stable or a situation in which we are responding so quickly that we can safely ignore all other factors.

Look Closer

At this point, it is essential to take a much closer look at what is actually happening in your environment. Few of us do this though as we get caught up by the momentum in stressful events.

Imagine there's trouble at work. Sales are beginning to drop. Resources will be getting scarce and our emotions are likely to be negative (you may be anxious and a little fearful), so you are more likely to conclude that you don't have enough time to look deeply. Instead, you speed up your revolution around the cycle. This is likely to increase the mismatch.

Taking time for each step becomes impossible. The fear of being overtaken exerts an influence: the elephant is agitated. You focus on doing, doing, doing instead of deepening your understanding and start to skip steps in an effort to keep up. This becomes frantic activity instead of meaningful action.

This frantic activity makes you vulnerable to mistakes and your results worsen. Eventually, the only possible actions in this now hostile environment are those of your deepest most ingrained habits. The environment is dishing out a beating, and it feels as if you are fighting for your life. Just at the time when the situation demands your best, you are at our worst. Then anger at what's happening builds and you may even take it out on those around you. This damages potential alliances.

Figure 12. How Stress Distorts Thinking

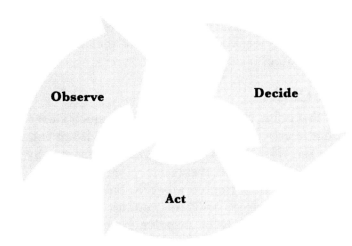

Orient

Observe   Decide

Act

This response is exactly what your opponent would want–if you had one. Your emotions are being governed by the energy and momentum of the situation and put an end to any genuine thinking—a bad place to be.

Einstein Wasn't Precise Enough

So what happened? What caused the isolation? The first problem was you were never really in touch in the first place. The "efficient" OODA cycle delivered good results as long as the factors you had fixed in your mind remained fixed in the environment. You were relying on old intelligence and were actually lucky to get good results for so long. It also shows that Einstein's oft quoted definition of insanity as "*doing the same thing and expecting a different result*,"[69] is not precise enough. In turbulent environments, you can pretty much guarantee a *different* result from doing the same thing. Insanity is actually doing the same thing and expecting *a better result*.

The next thing was that your emotions began to distort your perceptions. Emotional distortion restricts the data you can take in (to limit more bad news) which makes it impossible to have a full picture of reality. This made it easier for the elephant to run off down a negative path.

The best military leaders understand the thought processes of their opponents and *"get inside their decision cycle"* to quote Boyd. They then feed them unexpected or ambiguous information which makes them uncertain (and fearful) of the situation and their ability to tackle it. This reduces both desire and capacity. The experiences of the losing general were the same as our inexperienced paratroopers or you or me when we lose our direct connection with our environment. For us and the paratroopers, there is no malevolent opponent feeding the images, it all happens in our own minds as we stop paying attention to what is happening and focus instead on our (negative) judgment or reaction instead. This creates a vicious, self-propelled downward spiral.

Reconnect with Your Environment

The key to avoiding this isolation is to continuously assess and test your understanding of the environment. To create the time this takes, learn to anticipate events and conditions more successfully. Accurate anticipation will help you to understand the direction the situation is taking and then act in a way that improves the harmony between you and your environment. As Russ Ackoff used to point out, *if you can create the future, you don't need to predict it.*[70]

A Picture of Your Best Thought Process

How does this more skilled way of thinking and acting look? Well, even though the circular OODA I showed you is in every management book that mentions Boyd except one (Chet Richards's *Certain to Win*); Boyd never drew his OODA loop that way. Chet Richard's told me that he did sometimes describe it that way though so he deserves some of the credit/blame for the subsequent focus on it! However, my sense is that this was in the context of a slightly different situation where a skilled performer could act and get ahead of the events of the environment. This implies a dynamic and accurate understanding of the situation–something that is shown and not just implied in the full OODA diagram. (Also, Boyd's complete OODA approach is highly dynamic interactive process that is not necessarily sequential.)

This does not mean, however, that the circular loop is useless or wrong. As Boyd described in his last major presentation, *Conceptual Spiral*, and summarized in his densely packed four-page masterpiece, *The Essence of Winning and Losing,* the circular loop can be a model of learning. To use it safely in the appropriate context, we must remember it should be embedded it into the OODA "loop" depicted in Figure 13. Perhaps its greatest value is to remind us that if we want to thrive (or simply survive) the heat of conflict, we have to be learning about our environment (which in a conflict includes opponents) and be willing to experiment with new adaptations and additions to our existing repertoire.

Below is the actual diagram Boyd used to describe how someone is able to win, i.e. maintain independence to act and to make progress in any situation.[71]

It looks complicated when you first see it (one of the reasons why most people use the simplified version), so give yourself a few seconds to take it in. Start at the top line, read from left to right and then drop down and take in the rest of the detail.

A great deal of information is available at the observation stage if we are open to it. We can't perceive it all, so we prioritise what is most relevant based on what we have learned from previous situations. Most importantly, given the startling amount of potential data, we make crucial choices about what to ignore and then what to focus on.

This observation then feeds forward into our orientation. There are many different elements to this part of the process, such as previous experience and how we break down the information and then reassemble it (analysis and synthesis). Our previous experience has lots of different points of reference for us. Storing lots of old patterns, as well as our genetic heritage—what predisposes us to be effective or ineffective in some situations.

Taking all this together we make our decision and select an action from the myriad of possibilities. Interestingly, Chet Richards told me that Boyd had preferred *hypothesis* to *decide* because it left you in no doubt that we must always be exploring and testing.[72] This is worth remembering as you engage with your environment. Your understanding will never be complete, so each action is a potential opportunity to test what you think you know.

Figure 13. The Full OODA Diagram

(© Col. John R. Boyd estate)

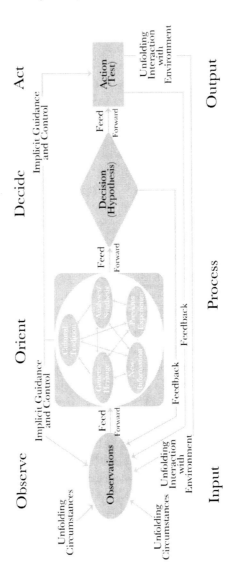

Most of the time, we would like our action to flow directly from our orientation via the "*implicit guidance and control*" link. In other words, most of the time, because of our previous experience and training, we "*just know what to do*" and can do it. Martial artists and maneuver warfare practitioners spend enormous amounts of time in training and exercises trying to ensure that they can utilize this link better than their opponents.

You can perhaps see more clearly why we focused so much developing mastery. With it, you can make the difficult simple and handle the higher stress levels inherent in turbulent situations.

It Can All Happen At Once

Boyd was clear that each stage could happen at the same time. It didn't have to happen in the order presented on the page. Remember he used OODA first to describe winning and losing in air-to-air combat–conflicts that rarely lasted longer than a minute. As one pilot moves into position, the opponent begins to respond causing a reaction from the other and so on. It's a 600 mph dance of action and reaction, of interaction and isolation.

To complete this model at speed and to address the apparent complications, Boyd stressed the importance of superior preparation ("Do your homework") and of making your understanding intuitive. This may have been the main value of the Aerial Attack Study, Boyd's assessment of competing fighter planes and all the potential moves and countermoves open to the pilot.

This awareness allowed pilots to prepare more effectively and to have a good idea of which types of moves would work best against a certain opponent. With mastery we are able to act quickly and decisively without hurrying and act using the "implicit guidance and control" steps in the diagram. You can be more open to a deeper connection with your environment. To free up the mental space to do this, you must have done your homework.

Boyd's work also reminds me of the importance of reducing the distance between thought and action. In turbulent environments, it's crucial to effectively combine the two. Here is what Argyris and Schon said about active inquiry and what they describe as the Deweyan inquirer [after the Pragmatist philosopher, John Dewey.]

> *"The Deweyan inquirer is not a spectator but an actor who stands within a situation of action, seeking actively to understand and change it."*[73]

Our Actions Change the Environment

Boyd also stressed again and again how your actions at every stage affect what is happening in the environment. Your presence changes the environment, and your actions start to change the environment you are trying to understand. You cannot not be a part of your environment and you cannot completely separate your actions with all the others going on around you. This is another reason why self-awareness is so important–you need to be able to figure out how you are affecting what you are observing and adjust accordingly. The best leaders I have worked with have all been able to put people at ease so that they behave as they would have had the leader not been there. This is essential if you want to understand what really happens in your business.

In certain competitive situations, our actions can have an enormous impact on the environment of our opponent. This can be the physical impact of a sporting contest that allows physical contact and the mental and emotional impact possible in non-contact endeavours where we can get inside our opponents decision making cycle. If you understand the decision your competitor is trying to make, you can change the external conditions/ information before they have chance to execute the decision. This slows them down as they have to recommence their deliberations which gives you a speed advantage.

How You Are Different at Your Best

To summarise this way of thinking, let's put ourselves back into the situation from the start of this chapter when sales started to drop.

On reflection, you had a sense that things were shifting for some time. Things were starting to feel different, and you were concerned you may be missing something. You focus first on the external environment. To ensure you really understand what is happening you look at results of your previous actions in this environment. What was the same? What was different? What surprised you? What whispers had you heard that may suggest a shift? Based on your previous decisions (hypotheses), what information should you pay more attention to next time? Are there any assumptions you want to test? What can you do to explore the changes?

Listen to the Quiet Voice of Change

Having heard this quiet voice of change, you persuade some colleagues to join you in a thorough market assessment. You talk about how the story or narrative in the market could evolve and you discuss the signals that would tell you things are changing. One colleague highlights a particular opportunity, so you agree to look out for that.

This time, as things continue to change, you spot one of the early, potential trends. A customer who used to be one of your biggest advocates no longer praises your products the way they did. In fact, one of your sales team said he even complained about something last month. So you visit the customer with one of the engineers who took part in the market assessment.

The meeting takes all day but you leave having promised to create a fast prototype of the kind of thing your client would like. You don't know how you are going to do it, but both you and your colleague are convinced it's an interesting opportunity and it fits one of the narratives you created for how the market could develop. You will be learning a lot, and there is no way your client is going anywhere now that he is advising you on the exciting, new product.

In this scenario, you are able to get ahead of the changes if you understand the present more successfully, build stronger alliances with key elements in your environment (your customer in this case), and run joint tests cutting costs and hopefully increasing your tempo. Much of this progress comes down to being able to hear and respond strongly to whispers or weak signals instead of having to wait for screams.

Karl Weick and Kathleen Sutcliffe talk about the importance of weak signals in their book, *Managing the Unexpected*:

> "*The overwhelming tendency is to respond to weak signals with a weak response. Mindfulness preserves the capability to see the significance of weak signals and to respond vigorously.*"[74]

The ability to hear whispers is a valuable and rare skill in dynamic situations. Cultivating the ability is worthwhile because it can give you precious time and availability of resources as we can perceive negative changes sooner before they become serious resource drains (such as quality problems on a production line). This superior listening makes any mid-course correction faster and cheaper, and enables you to spot opportunities before the competition.

In addition to more perceptive listening, what else can you do to apply the wisdom in and behind Boyd's OODA loop? We will take the rest of the chapter to answer that question.

10a.
Ways to Apply Boyd's Insights

Remain Open and Curious

Remain open to what is happening. Get curious about what you do and don't know. Nearly all of us dramatically overestimate how well we understand our environment and we underestimate the role of chance or fortune in the results we get.[75] Maintaining the sense that your decisions are really hypotheses about what will or won't happen if you do x or y is a great way to counteract this. If you have only a hypothesis, then it is important to remain open to better descriptions and predictors of emerging trends and patterns.

Go to the Margins and See for Yourself

The next thing is to review and strengthen your connections with your external environment. What are you doing to renew those connections? How much joint working do you do with your customers to create a shared view of what is happening? How strong are those connections? Where are the most significant matches and mismatches between you and your environment (either as an individual or as an organisation)? What are you doing to see the changes for yourself?

Sir Terry Leahy, former CEO of Tesco's, one of the world's most successful retailers, spent a great deal of time with customers. He insisted on observing focus groups himself, so that he could get their unedited comments. Another UK retailer, Sir Ken Morrison, characteristically avoided the cost of focus groups and simply spent time in his stores. He would pepper customers with questions about why they bought one thing instead of another as he packed their bags. His stores were the best I have ever seen. He managed to inculcate in his employees a similar sense of what customers do and don't like and a desire to remain open and curious to what they may want tomorrow.

Michael Dell, of Dell Computers, used to spend two to three days a week with customers seeing and hearing for himself what was going on. The whispers that help you discern the future direction of your environment are being spoken at the margins now. Hear these whispers before your competition does. Senior teams get blind-sided often because they think their job is to tell when it is really to first listen and understand. So get out of your office and get people to tell you what they really think instead of what they think you want to hear.

Increase Your Tests

How can you increase the number and quality of tests that you perform? As turmoil increases, it becomes much more expensive to run enough tests to get the best ideas. Working with other firms (or individuals) and sharing the results means you can effectively perform many more relevant tests. How can you engage colleagues or other non-competing organizations working in similar environments?

If you begin with what you think you know, you can start looking for contradictory evidence. Once you are certain, you can begin pushing out from solid ground to areas where you are less confident.

Michael Roberto in *Know What You Don't Know* says one of the most important and most difficult skills for a leader is to work out not the answers to problems but to actually find what the problems are.[76] This insight came from a conversation with Robert McNamara, the former Secretary of Defence and businessman. Whilst giving a talk, McNamara told Roberto that Harvard should focus less on teaching problem solving techniques (the topic of

Roberto's first book) and focus more on teaching problem finding techniques because they were more important and more difficult.

Understand and Challenge Assumptions

Something that can blind us to the problems we face is invisible and untested assumptions. Gary Klein, leader in intuitive thinking, worked a great deal with the USMC. His work is stunning. One exercise he recommends in *The Power of Intuition* is the *Pre-Mortem,* which works well with individuals and brilliantly with teams.[77]

Conduct a Pre-Mortem

We know that post-mortems are conducted when something or someone has died unexpectedly. By contrast, the pre-mortem prepares a team for a challenge/project launch by having the team imagine the project has died a horrible death and identifying all the possible causes. This exercise effectively surfaces key and often unspoken assumptions. Here's how Klein describes it in his excellent book:

1. Imagine that your project has just suffered a total failure. All hell is breaking loose. What could have possibly happened to cause this? On your own, list all the possible reasons why the project failed.
2. Draw out all the reasons (in turn) from each person, giving one reason at a time and getting them all out on a board that people can see.
3. Revisit your plan and adapt any actions as you see fit.
4. Review this list as you successfully execute the project to ensure you remain on track.

Klein stressed to me that Step 3 can be demoralizing as there are often many reasons why something could fail. He suggests going round the room and asking each participant to think of one thing they can do personally to ensure a particular thing never occurs. That way, they reconnect with all the ways they can influence what could happen and the exercise inspires instead of demoralises.

I have found this to be a fantastic exercise for individuals, too, when we are performing a turnaround. It is essential to consider in advance the things that could go wrong and why someone may not be successful. Doing this in advance helps people to anticipate and prepare for the possible eventualities, further increasing the likelihood of success. If and when set-backs happen, they know what to do immediately. Some even enjoy the challenge.

Worry Less About Yourself

If you are concerned first with understanding something more deeply, you are less concerned about the potential impact on you and you more likely to refrain from any judgments. This makes it easier to temper any emotional reactions you may experience. We become emotional only when we focus internally. Not being too concerned about the impact on you is hard. It gets easier if you focus on building the ability and confidence to know that you'll be OK whatever the impact. And remind yourself that if something is still in motion there are still ways to influence its trajectory. Your interactions could be the crucial factor in shifting things back towards your intention so you must keep fighting.

Don't Ever Rely on Things Getting Better

Speaking of clients in trouble, in the initial conversation with a prospective turnaround client, some say to me:

"Well, it can't get any worse."

When you are dealing with difficulty, a belief that you can still make a difference or that things can get better is crucial. However, being delusional prompts you to waste resources attempting things with no chance of success. So when would believing that things will get better make things easier? And when could it make it worse?

Emotions distort your ability to accurately assess risk.[78] When relaxed, you tend to underestimate the potential hazard and overestimate your capacity to deal with it. When experiencing negative emotions (fear, anxiety, etc.) you do the reverse–make the hazard look bigger than it is and underestimate your ability to tackle it. However, my response to someone declaring that things can't get any worse is usually something like:

> *"You probably think things can't get any worse because the stress is limiting your imagination. I can say with utter certainty that things can always get worse. You can't afford that kind of delusional, wishful thinking if you want to get out this trouble."*

Why would I say that when I am committed to developing confident, courageous clients? The hope that things can't or won't get any worse may have been keeping them going. I am not trying to damage their confidence, but to build it up on solid foundations. To do that, I need to stop them being optimistic about the wrong things.

Be Optimistic About Your Ability to Recover

So, instead of allowing clients to take false solace in the situation not getting worse, I offer them solace of a more robust kind:

"Don't focus on things getting better. Focus on you getting better! I want to help you see that even if things get worse, there are still ways for you to recover and even come back stronger."

Most people when they face trouble try to minimize the size of the challenge. They don't think to focus on the other side of the basic stress equation (*perception of challenge > perception of resources*) to see just how much more they can handle and do if they were more resourceful.

The focus on trying to play down the size of the challenge distorts our view of a situation. This makes it impossible for us to anticipate and prepare effectively. To make matters worse, people who are supposed to help us to prepare for these situations often play down the challenge and lie to us too in a sincere, but utterly unhelpful attempt to keep our spirits up.

Lying and Childbirth: A Global Conspiracy?

A great example of well-meaning dishonesty is childbirth and the first 12 months of taking care of a baby. I haven't actually experienced the former (obviously), but my wife has and I have done the latter twice.

Caring for a baby in the first 12 months is easily the hardest thing I have ever done. I love my kids and having them is amazing. However, had either baby been my actual employer and did the same things, they would be in prison for the torture of constant sleep deprivation and their impossible demands! Instead of jail time, they got more fluffy teddies, lots of hugs, and their parents got to experience temporary insanity. But we got through it. And it showed that when you have sufficient purpose, your powers of endurance can be utterly amazing.

Had someone told us how hard it was going to be, we could have prepared more effectively. Instead we hit a wall and thought that the trouble must be down to something we were doing wrongly. Instead we had been lied to by well–meaning, but misguided helpers.

It's much better to give someone a realistic assessment of the challenge and to then focus on increasing their powers of resilience and recovery. For example, healthcare professionals could say something like:

> "Other than a life threatening car accident or something similar, childbirth is likely to be the most painful thing a woman experiences. Thankfully, women are designed to handle this and they have an utterly amazing ability to recover. And thanks to advances in medicine, you are pretty much guaranteed to get through it. Also, the actual birth hardly ever lasts for more than a few hours and the most intense pain doesn't last that long (but it may feel like an eternity at the time). The mothers I've spoken to all say that it was worth the effort. The other great thing is that the right preparations can reduce this challenge further. Would you like to look at that now?"

If we had more conversations like that, parents can know what's coming and still be confident they will get through it (as we do). As Carl Rogers said, *"Facts are always friendly."*[79]

Knowing your limits and what you can achieve with your current resources makes you better at asking for help when it is clear you can't achieve your goals on your own. That's what I help my clients achieve. I think they appreciate the reality and the support.

This common but flawed approach of focusing on the wrong side of the equation (on reducing the size of the challenge) also explains an idea that has become popular through the work of leading management thinker, Jim Collins.

The Stockdale Paradox Is No Paradox

Author Jim Collins, in *Good to Great*,[80] describes something he calls the *Stockdale Paradox*. He named this after Vice Admiral James Stockdale who was the highest ranking POW in the Vietnam War. Prison conditions were horrific. Stockdale explained to Collins that it was the optimists who died. They believed they'd be out by Christmas and couldn't handle it when things got worse instead of better. Stockdale said that he believed he would get out and make something positive from the experience. Consequently, he was willing to confront the harsh reality of spending years as a POW (he was imprisoned for seven and a half years).

From this, Collins created the Stockdale Paradox:

Retain faith that you will prevail in the end regardless of the difficulties	AND at the same time	Confront the most brutal facts of your current reality, whatever they might be.

James Stockdale is one of the greatest leaders I have ever studied, so if he says that he never doubted that he would get out, then I can't disagree fully. Yet, having read what he wrote at the time, I don't know how he could have believed that.

Stockdale wrote a fantastic book of essays, *Thoughts of a Philosophical Fighter Pilot*, which addressed what he called "*crucibles*"–situations where you "*grow or die.*" In the book, he mentions Viktor Frankl, who survived the Nazi concentration camps and wrote *Man's Search for Meaning.* Frankl seems to have been the inspiration for Stockdale's comments to Collins. In *Thoughts*, Stockdale says:

He [Frankl] says that the big threats to morale in the crucible are not the pessimists but the incurable vocal persistent optimists.[81]

My aim is not to lessen Stockdale's achievements. I think Stockdale actually did something more remarkable than living the Stockdale Paradox as Collins defines it. He managed to take something from the experience at the time, even when he was being tortured. He focused on his available resources and on his own resourcefulness in dealing with whatever was done to him. He created a narrative that did not demand that he had to survive to still make progress or to "*win.*" Then he set to work serving his men. This for me is a much greater level of optimism than keeping your spirits up in the face of a truly shocking reality.

Just How Optimistic Was Stockdale Really?

For the first four years of his seven and a half year imprisonment, Stockdale was tortured routinely and kept in near permanent isolation. Probably the best example of just how optimistic and strong he was happened during that period. After four years of imprisonment, Stockdale tried to take his own life.

He didn't do it out of personal desperation [his strength and endurance were utterly staggering]; he did it to make progress in his mission–protecting his men.

The guards had caught him with a note giving instructions to his resistance group. One of the lessons Stockdale learned from being tortured was that you can endure torture without revealing any meaningful secrets as long as your torturer doesn't know where to look. If your guards know where to probe, then you'll break–either physically or mentally.

In the next torture session (as they had his note) he knew he would either be broken physically and killed or give up his men. Given the skill and experience of the torturer, being killed was unlikely. And as he had inadvertently given them a clue as to what to ask, he knew he would break. Having thought this through, he saw that that his best option for serving his primary duty of protecting his men was to take his own life. So that is what he tried to do without hesitation.

The Stockdale's story [his wife was an amazing woman and led the wife's of the POWs] has inspired me in many ways. What James Stockdale did in that particular crucible is one of the most extraordinary examples of leadership I have ever come across. So I do agree with Collins that what he calls the "*Stockdale Paradox*" may be one of the greatest lessons any of us could strive to integrate in our lives. But I believe it isn't a paradox at all. This is what I think Stockdale was talking about when he said he knew *he* would prevail:

> *There was a special personal commitment in Alcatraz [their POW camp]. It was unity over self, no matter what the cost. Joseph Conrad could have been describing the Gang [his team]: "A certain readiness to perish is not so very rare, but it is seldom that you meet men whose souls, steeled in the impenetrable armor of resolution, are ready to fight a losing battle to the last."*[82]

Stockdale knew his chances of survival were low and that being killed was more likely than survival. But he could be confident that at least one of his gang would survive. He also knew that living or dying was ultimately out of his control. As a serving officer, his job was to disrupt the Vietnamese war effort and help his men to resist their captors as much as was humanly possible. That he and many of his team survived such an ordeal is an extraordinary testimony to the courage, strength, and leadership they showed. To survive, they had to live for each other and care less and less about themselves. If you live with that attitude, you don't have to survive physically to prevail. Their warrior code and values would prevail even if they didn't. So if you are facing difficulty, don't rely on things getting better. Accept the situation in all its bleakness and then get fighting with everything you have. Even if it doesn't make a difference to you, it could make a difference to someone else.

Thankfully most of us do not have to face such challenging situations so let's get back to dealing with day–to–day activities.

Stick to the Facts

Earlier in the book, I mentioned the benefits of changing the catchphrase of the TV show Dragnet, "*Just the facts, Ma'am*," to "*Just the stress, thanks.*" Well, we are now returning to the original. This is essential when you want to control your thoughts. We find ourselves in trouble when we piece together a series of facts and then make an erroneous conclusion, for which we just don't have the data. Uncertainty makes us nervous and anxious so we often make unhelpful conclusions instead of enduring more uncertainty as we establish what is really going on. Instead of hasty conclusions practice saying (and accepting), "*I just don't know, but I'm interested to find out.*"

It amazes me that otherwise supportive and encouraging people can say things to themselves (in their heads) that they would be horrified to say to anyone else. To reduce this, take a day to verbalise everything that you say to yourself about your actions (out of ear shot of others). This can be so shocking that it prompts clients to take the action to calm the voices in their minds. A slightly softer alternative is to write down what you are saying to yourself and then review it for factual inaccuracies. Focus on the difference between fact and assertion.

In our understanding of a situation, we go wrong when we fail to make the distinction between the facts of a situation and our conclusions or judgments about where it may go next. The facts will always help in the end as they highlight mismatches and help you to understand what is actually happening. We just need to ensure we have the resources to handle it. As you review your comments to yourself, check for facts that quickly morph into unsupported assertions or extrapolations.

If the dialogue in your head is not helpful then you need to calmly and firmly address it, the way you would address the comments of an anxious child with an over-active imagination. Eventually, if you do that enough, the negative self-talk lessens, and you will be able to allow occasional chatter without responding.

You Just Don't Know What You Can Do

I spend my professional and personal life helping people do things they thought were impossible/lost forever. I have seen seemingly ordinary people do utterly amazing things. Even with all those data points and experience, I refuse to predict someone's potential. If someone wants to achieve a level of performance they have previously never achieved I ensure we focus on what would have to happen for that to become reality. What environment would they need? What actions would they need to be doing every day and for how long? What do they need to ensure they get that time to build the momentum that will deliver those results?

Do you need to believe that anything is possible to go for that promotion or start that diet? How can that be anything but delusional thinking? If you are simply willing to give it everything and be open to doubt, you can apply this factual approach with a slightly positive spin and you'll be ready for whatever comes your way.

Getting Forensic About Your Thoughts

David Rock, in his book, *Your Brain at Work*,[83] shares research that supports the findings of the paratrooper study. He highlights the error of trying to suppress emotions. He encourages his readers to recognize and accept their emotional state. He focuses on two activities–labelling and reappraising. These are core skills and are worth developing enough so that you can perform them both at speed.

First Label What You Are Experiencing

Rock quotes one study, where two subjects had a conversation and one had to suppress an emotion. They measured the blood pressure of each and found that the person suppressing their emotion caused the blood pressure of the observer to increase. As Rock points out, *"suppression literally makes other people uncomfortable."*[84]

The HeartMath team would have a deeper perspective on this that isn't mentioned in Rock's book. Emotional suppression causes incoherent heart rhythms and the waves coming off your heart and head as a result of that will be strong enough to affect the rhythms of other people around you. This can stimulate feelings of discomfort in another.

Rock suggests you notice the emotions you are experiencing. Then label them and express this description as much as the situation permits. Sometimes, it may be that you can't say anything about feeling disappointed, angry, or upset. In which case, simply notice to yourself. This then allows you to ask a question we covered earlier, *"What next?"*

Take a break if you need to, or carry on as sometimes the labelling is all you need to do. The point is not to have some kind of therapy session but to quickly notice that you are experiencing x or y and then focus on what you can do about it right now. Remember emotions, at their core, are sources of energy designed to help achieve some outcome so a redirection to a more helpful outcome deals with the energy and helps you to win.

Accepting and Reappraising

Accepting the emotional state you are in is easier if you see it as perfectly normal given the circumstances. When helping people through difficult transitions I warn them of the erratic progress everyone makes as they turn things around:

> "*Some days you'll wake up feeling strong and positive, other days you won't. This is a perfectly normal part of the recovery process. If you accept this, you can experience just the stress of that situation and minimize the total size of the stress curve. You don't have to waste energy worrying you're about to relapse or get angry with yourself for not being cured. Embrace the tough day, address your emotional state, and remember it will pass.*"

Rock calls this process *normalising*.

Control Your Comparisons: Monty Python

I grew up in Yorkshire, a particularly beautiful part of the UK (if that's where you're from!) One of my favourite Monty Python sketches was the *Yorkshiremen Sketch*. Four successful Yorkshiremen are sitting back after a fine dinner and they try to outdo each other on how hard their lives were growing up. The characters go from being grateful to having the money for a cup of tea to living in a cardboard box, to getting up before they went to sleep and paying for the luxury of "*workin' darn mill.*"

Control your comparisons both positively and negatively. Most of the time we are making relative judgments about whether something is hard or easy, good or bad, positive or negative and we invariably compare our performance/situation with people who have more than we do. Get into the habit of asking "*Compared to what?*" and "*How helpful is this comparison?*" And ensure the comparison takes in the whole data set (including those below you). For example, if you are ever bothered about your salary being lower than the top performer in your industry, see how your salary ranks globally at www.globalrichlist.com. I guarantee you'll be amazed by how rich you really are.

One of the reasons why I love working with servicemen and women is that in any *"I've had it tough"* competition they can beat me without even trying. That helps me to see my problems for what they are.

Control Your Comparisons: Tri for Akio

In the chapter on movement, I suggested doing something physical for charity. In 2011, I completed two triathlons in a week to raise money for Great Ormond Street Children's Hospital in London. My personal reason for supporting GOSH came from one of my university tutors, Yoko Sellek, who had lost her son, Akio, an extraordinary young man, to a particularly nasty illness. Akio was treated at GOSH for 14 years of his 16 year life.

Yoko is one of the strongest people I know, and I wanted to honour the effort that Akio, her family, and the amazing team at GOSH had made. I have some very generous friends and I managed to raise $6000. All I had to do was complete the challenge.

The first triathlon (an Olympic distance event involving a 1.5km swim, 40km bike, and 10km run) went brilliantly in near perfect conditions. I set a new personal best and was really eager to do the second event the following week—the much tougher half-Ironman.

The distance of that race was a 1.9km swim, 90km cycle and then a half-marathon (21km) in the beautiful but rugged New Forest in the South of England. The swim went extremely well and I set my fastest ever time. After that, though, things went downhill rapidly. I had trouble on the bike and never got comfortable. The previous event had clearly taken a lot out of my legs, and I began to fully appreciate why people had been so supportive—doing two triathlons in a week is a foolish and painful thing to do!

The cycle took nearly an hour longer than I had hoped, and I stepped off the bike in a foul mood. The thought of running a half marathon after nearly four hours of strenuous exercise left me feeling sick. It was much harder than I had anticipated. Out of ear shot of any other racer, I cursed and felt sorry for myself. I even thought of stopping. And then I controlled my comparisons and the dialogue when something like this:

Jon, this half marathon is not going to be easy. You're tired and you're clearly not at your best [accept the reality of where you are]. But stopping isn't for you. What would you tell Yoko when you had to give the money back—"Sorry, I felt tired..." She may not judge you but you should judge yourself. This is in honour of Akio and the courage he and everyone around him showed [reminding myself of the bigger purpose and controlling the comparison]. Besides, it is only 21km. You're not doing an Ironman [that's a full marathon]— so it could be worse [CYC]. Sure, it's harder than you thought it was going to be, but you have trained well.

And finishing is the goal, not winning. You're not in that bad a shape, so at your worse you will be able to walk this in 3 hours. That's all you have to do. So get moving.

And that's what I did. It took me a couple more miles to clear the negative emotions (hormones take a while to shift even when you are running). After that I even enjoyed some of the walk/jog through the New Forest. It only took 2.5 hours too. Finishing felt amazing–as did the celebratory drinks with Yoko and Akio's consultant, the amazing Paul Brogan.

Create a Challenge List

So, how can you use this strategy on a regular basis? When we face the challenge of rectifying a negative mismatch, we often compare it to a normal day. This makes it difficult by comparison. But will it be that hard compared to all the other things you have done in your life? How hard will it be then?

When you are having a decent day, take some time to write down the hardest things you have faced in your life. Write down what made them tough, how you felt at the time, and what you did to overcome them. Pay particular attention if that challenge was the toughest thing you have ever had to face.

Talk to people who know you well and saw how much the event stretched you. They can give you a perspective on just how much fuss you made or how much courage you showed to do what you needed to do.

Review this list periodically to remind yourself just how tough you can be when pressed. Then when you face another challenge, compare it and your emotional state to what you are experiencing now. If you have never faced anything as hard, then you are in a crucible, as Jim Stockdale, would describe it. Then you get to earn your PhD in difficult situations!

Having said that, you will have had plenty of "*toughest thing I have ever faced*" situations so that part isn't new. Your amygdala will appreciate the reminder. In those times, you probably doubted your ability to come back and will have wondered if you had the resources to deal with it. This is a helpful reminder when you are wondering the same thing this time. As you found the ability and the resources, you can legitimately ask, "*Why is this situation going to be different?*" or "*What did I do to find the resources I needed?*" Then get to work.

When You Don't Have the Resources

And if you didn't have the resources the last time, all that tells you is that you need to be sure to get them this time! And this is a time when looking at someone else's tough list really helps—look at the people who amaze you with their fortitude and strength of character. It's one reason why I love reading about amazing people such as James Stockdale, or spending time with service members and other inspirational people. They've had to endure extraordinary challenges and most seem like normal people. So what's to say you couldn't do something similar if you had to? Experiencing pain right now does not mean your suffering will go on forever. There are worse things than experiencing pain every now and then.

Chrissie Wellington, World's Best Athlete?

An excellent example of someone who used other people's challenges to inspire her to unprecedented achievement is Chrissie Wellington, the British Ironman triathlete who retired from competition in 2012 as the only undefeated professional triathlete in Ironman history. [An ironman is a 140.2 mile race of swimming, cycling and running.]

In her autobiography,[85] there is a chapter entitled *"The Heroes of Ironman."* She briefly mentions the great champions who have gone before (as you'd expect) but she then gets to her real heroes, people who have faced much bigger challenges than a sporting race.

For example, she speaks of Doug and Rick Hoyt: Rick is a quadriplegic and Doug, his father, tows him as he completes Ironman races; Scott Rigsby, who is the first double-leg amputee to complete an ironman; and Jane Tomlinson, the inspirational British cancer fighter who was given six months to live when her cancer returned a third time. Jane raised millions of pounds for cancer charities by completing endurance races before she succumbed to the illness seven years later. These people help Chrissie reduce the size of the challenge–an Ironman can't be that hard if you have all your limbs and don't have cancer!

In 2011, Chrissie completed what she considered to be her perfect race when she overcame a serious training injury and came from behind to win her fourth World title. She said that she had never encountered such challenge before and had to dig deeper than she had imagined possible. Undoubtedly, she had some "training secrets" and had staggering powers of endurance, but her biggest secret, for me, was her deeper sense of purpose woven into her ferocious will. She was and still is connected to deeper and greater levels of inspiration than her competitors, and when it really mattered, she could draw on that. She had a bigger why and cared more about others so she could care less about herself. A true champion and the sport is poorer for her retirement.

Focus on Why

This connects with another Stockdale insight I have experienced in a much less traumatic situation. Your endurance and stress tolerance is affected massively by your motivations. Striving for someone else's benefit and knowing that the other person is doing the same for you makes it possible to endure things you previously thought were unimaginable. This may sound extreme and unusual but my research into first responders and military personnel shows that this attitude is reassuringly present in lots of places (even if it is sadly rare in business). **WIIFM (What's in it for me) is the most boring radio station in the world**. That we indulge ourselves so much focusing on it does not service to ourselves or the people who helped us to achieve what we have.

You need *capacity and desire.* In some situations, we don't run out of physical energy, we run out of mental and moral energy, our desire or motivation. And the greater the significance of your answer to the *why,* the more you'll be able to stand. So if you are having some trouble, remind yourself why you are doing it.

One of the reasons why so many people are suffering from workplace stress is that too many leaders have inadvertently stripped away any greater purpose to work than striving to make next quarter's numbers. Helping shareholders who show no long term commitment to the company is not motivating.

Cultivating Perspective

Turbulent situations distort our perspective. Instead of seeing how everything fits together and seeing the momentum and stream of events all you have is the *infernal now.* If you can see something as a blip or a bump in the road instead of a career-ending catastrophe, you can usually keep your emotions in check. And, even if you do experience a massive career crash, there will be something else after it. There always is. As Tom Hank's character says in Charlie Wilson's War, " *The ball keeps bouncing.* " And it is usually what happens before and then after a career-changing event that determines what you will make of it.

One thing in Lance Armstrong's favour as his world has crashed around his ears is the knowledge that he had been through worse. He has a personal comparison that could help him to face up to the toughest aspects of accepting all the times he lied and abused people.

And This Too Will Pass

Finally, going back to the research from the paratroopers, putting a time limit on the challenge makes a difference. When will we be safe again?

And focusing on how far you have travelled helps. An interesting piece of research by Bob Cialdini, the world's leading authority on influence, showed that it's better to focus on the smaller percentage of our journey through a difficult time or task. That is, if the task is less than 50% complete, you remind yourself of your distance from the start, "*I'm 20% of the way there.*" When you are over half way heading towards the finish, focus on how much there is left "*Only 20% left!*"

Sometimes there is no known end point. My mother helped me with that as I worked through my challenges. One thing she reminded me of was something she had taken from the Bible:

> *"Jon, in the Bible, it often says, "And so it came to pass..." At no point does it say, "And so it came to stay..."*

I took solace in this. It helped me to carry on for a little longer when I thought I couldn't go any further. At times it did feel as if the trouble would stick around forever but better times have returned. I still honour the wisdom of this insight. When times are bad, I work to hasten its departure. When times are good, I appreciate what I have.

I hope you find these ideas helpful. Together with the work you have done to master the moment and increase your capacity for challenge and recovery, they will help you remain focused on the task at hand. In the final section of the book I am going to focus on how you can increase the care and support you give and get by gaining greater influence over your emotional state. You've got 10% left!

Summary

- Boyd's most famous work is the Observe-Orient-Decide-Act loop which describes how someone interacts with their environment to maximise their chances of winning.
- The popular way of depicting the loop breaks the single most important point of increasing and improving interaction with your environment.
- The weaker our connection to and awareness of our external environment, the more vulnerable we are to viral stupidity. Left unchecked it can prompt faster and faster cycles of thoughtless action.
- Boyd preferred the term "*hypothesis*" to "*decide*" as it ensures we remember our conclusions can only be temporary in a dynamic situation.
- To maintain our intelligence, we need to see the OODA process as a dynamic interaction between all four distinctive but not distinct activities.
- Each activity affects all the others and all can happen at the same time.
- It is also important to appreciate how our actions affect our environment even when we attempt to be detached or collect "objective" data.

- We can improve our orientation if we get to the margins and seek contrary information to challenge our hypotheses about how we can win. We cultivate our ability to hear the whispers of change instead of waiting for the screams.
- To maintain our openness to reality we need to have sufficient confidence that we can succeed in some way.
- Instead of trying to minimise the size of the challenge, we can emulate Jim Stockdale and build reality based confidence in our ability and desire to tackle the challenges we face.
- To help keep our thinking clear, it's helpful to control our comparisons both on what we have done before and what other people like us have faced.
- We can increase our endurance by focusing on why we are doing something as it directly affects our desire to see things through.

11.
Care and Support

As I have stressed throughout this book, emotions are crucial to your performance in challenging situations. In this final chapter, I am going to explore in more detail how you can consciously stimulate positive emotions for yourself and those around you. Doing this will make you and your team more resilient and resourceful and help to create the safe social environment. All this will allows you to really stretch and engage positively with the turbulence you experience.

The Creation of Positive Psychology

There are few people who could make a legitimate claim to have created a whole branch of psychology. Martin Seligman is one. He articulated the new field of positive psychology in 1998 to complement the traditional field of psychology that had focused mainly on mental illness. Seligman and a few other pioneers suggested that it may be worthwhile studying and nurturing psychological flourishing.[86] Given the latest advances in other scientific fields, this is now gathering tremendous energy and momentum.

Create "Positive Affect"

If there was one academic paper I could put in front of every leader or parent I think it would be one on human flourishing by Barbara Fredrickson and Marcial Losada.[87] It is utterly brilliant in its findings and in the rigor in which they uncover their conclusions about the impact and importance of positive emotions.[88]

In their article, they introduce the positivity ratio, which is the ratio between the times you experience positive emotions (from the right hand quadrants) such as compassion, contentment, gratitude, hope, interest, etc. versus negative emotions from the left-hand quadrants such as anger, fear, guilt, sadness, etc. The ratio between them is crucial for success.

According to the authors, a ratio of 3-1 (positive-negative) leads to flourishing which is, "*Living within an optimal range of human functioning, one that connotes goodness, generativity, growth and resilience.*" Below that, you may drift toward languishing: "*a disorder intermediate along the mental health continuum experienced by people who describe their lives as "hollow" or "empty."*"

The study found that this ratio is non-linear, meaning that a ratio of 2–1 doesn't give you 2/3 of the effect of a 3–1 ratio. If you have the lower ratio, you may enjoy no real benefit. Three and above brings a "*flourishing*" response, as if you have broken out of a negative gravitational force.

Positivity Broadens the Mind

Fredrickson and Losada argue that positive focus broadens your mind and makes you healthier in the long run. This has been a consistent theme of Fredrickson's work over many years, which she calls "*broaden and build.*"[89] Positive emotions stimulate the neurotransmitter dopamine. Dopamine connects parts of your brain allowing you to be creative and to come up with new solutions to problems. It also helps you to increase or build the resources (and resourcefulness) you have available.

Negative emotions, however, impede dopamine production (and other hormones essential for peak performance. This lack of dopamine makes creativity impossible as your brain doesn't have the building blocks to connect the synapses.

Positive emotions can literally build you up. For example, the hormone DHEA, produced when you experience positive emotions, is an essential building block for the anabolic hormones testosterone (in men) and estrogen (in women). DHEA is a great counteracting force to Cortisol and your DHEA-Cortisol ratio, one of the simplest measures of stress, could be seen as a simple positivity ratio at a hormonal level.

Why Do We Need a 3-1 Ratio to Flourish?

Why 3-1? This is a good question and there wasn't a wholly conclusive answer. However, the researchers point out that one unit of positive and one unit of negative are not the same. In evolutionary and hormonal terms, one negative experience needs to be more powerful and more immediate than a positive experience. There are evolutionary benefits to this. The negative focus helps you to quickly focus on problems (which may be life threatening). When something potentially negative happens, the fight-flight response gives you more than enough energy to get through (to be on the safe side).

Nothing bad is likely to happen from a positive event so an under-reaction to the positive event is unlikely to cause you problems. An under-reaction to a negative situation that turns out to be a lethal threat is dangerous, so your systems minimise the chance of that happening.

The impact of positive emotions builds over time. Again, this seems to be appropriate from an evolutionary perspective. Positive focus rewards over the longer term as it facilitates such things as creativity, innovation, and collaboration. Short term, the benefits are present but less pronounced.

Positivity in Teams: Create a Safe Environment

Marcial Losada has also completed interesting work that offers guidance for creating the safe social environment Professor Porges research shows is so important for high performance. Losada completed research into highest-performing business teams (as determined by conventional business measures). He established three key factors that differentiated them from average and poor performing teams.

- **Positivity-negativity:** A higher ratio of positive comments (expressing support, encouragement, or appreciation) to negative comments (expressing disapproval, sarcasm, or cynicism).
- **Inquiry-Advocacy:** The frequency that someone asks questions about someone's position on a topic or the times they say something supporting their own position.
- **Other-self:** The split between comments referring to self (themselves, the people present, or their company) and others (anyone else).

Losada's research showed the same 3-1 ratio was needed for flourishing to occur (actually 2.9-1). The top teams had a 5.6-1 ratio. It's vital to note that these positive comments were sincere and authentic. Even when top teams are disagreeing they tend to do it in an agreeable way (criticize the idea but take what they can from it whilst showing support for the individual). This brings me to two important caveats.

Two Important Caveats

Another reassuring element of the study was that the researchers wisely point out the benefits to being appropriately negative. Positivity must be grounded in reality.

According to Fredrickson and Losada, the positivity benefit peaked at an 11-1 ratio. In another paper, the authors make the analogy that if you can jump really high in the gym you could crash into the ceiling.

They also suggest that some forms of negativity are more helpful than others. For example, engaged disagreement in the topic instead of disgust or dismissal of the speaker would be two contrasting examples of helpful negativity and unhelpful negativity. You can say a lot more about someone's behaviour and have them accept it if they feel accepted as individuals. "*You're on the team. We want you on the team. And today your behaviour sucked,*" is the kind of negative feedback you want people to hear. (Even if you don't say the first two sentences, they need to feel it).

The other caveat will come as no surprise. Sincere negativity was found to be less unhelpful than faked positivity.[90] So, in case you need another reminder—suppression doesn't work! If you feel negative emotions, it's helpful to express them in a way that does no damage to others, and then to find a positive way to resolve either the feelings—a reframe may be in order—and/or to solve the problem. On the best teams, colleagues tend to help each other with this.

The goal is honest, constructive expression, and connection to reality. False positives give you the worst of both worlds. Uncertainty caused by insincere positivity is almost impossible to address because the person usually thinks he or she is helping and often gets upset when their contribution is not appreciated.

Balancing Confidence with Humility

When looking at team communication, and balancing confident expression of your ideas with an openness to others, it can be helpful to remember that anything you are doing is your *current best practice*. Given the VUCA nature of our environment [volatile, uncertain, complex and ambiguous], all ideas have a shelf life–a shelf life that is getting shorter. Far too many people forget that "*current*" is the word to emphasise. It is today's best practice. It's not the best practice for the rest of history.

When talking with others, share your best approach or practice, and then invite or even demand feedback and ideas on how to make it even better. This allows you to balance evidence-based confidence and humility.

Raise SEA Levels

There are benefits to increasing the sincere experience and expression of the positive behaviours that Fredrickson and Losada measured. To recap, these behaviours were amusement, awe, compassion, contentment, gratitude, hope, interest, joy, love, pride. So look for ways to experience more of those emotions. For now, we will focus on support, encouragement, and appreciation. These were ones that Losada looked for in his team study. They are also the positive emotions that come up most frequently in other studies.

To help my clients remember, I encourage them to *raise SEA levels.* I will be focusing on ways to do this for others but it is also important that you support, encourage, and appreciate what you do. So feel free to apply any of the exercises to yourself.

Offering Thanks: Large and Small

Sir Isaac Newton once said, "*If I have been able to see further, it was only because I stood on the shoulders of giants.*"[91] In my seminars, I ask people "*Who has helped you get to where you are today?*" meaning "*On whose shoulders are you standing?*"

I take them through the following five questions, and I invite you to do the same, recording your answers in your notebook. The more time you take on this, the more likely you will be to access the emotion that they triggered in you. Aim to feel the original appreciation or gratitude as you do the exercise.

Think of someone who helped you at an important time in your life. Take a few rhythmical, coherent breaths and consider the following questions.

1. What did the person help you to do?
2. What did they do that helped you?
3. What difference did they make?
4. Had you not received this help, what difference would it have made to your life?
5. If that person were here, what would you say to them?

Writing down your answers seems to make it easier to access the emotions and deepens your sense of connection with the person you are thinking about. Another way to deepen it even more is to write a letter or card to that person to tell them how much you appreciated their help. If they are still alive send it to them, if not write to their family.

In Praise of Pauline Nicholls

When I was first did this exercise, I thought of my swimming coach, a wonderful lady called Pauline Nicholls. Pauline coached me for about twelve years. When I spoke to my mother about her she pointed out that Pauline had helped in lots of other ways during my childhood. She was probably the most significant caring adult outside of my family who raised my SEA levels, especially when I was feeling down.

Pauline was the classroom assistant in my first year at school. She helped me to become a swimming coach, which was my first experience of coaching others. When I took a year to travel around Australia before university, she introduced me to some friends, Jill and Bryan Carter. They helped me to deal with some trouble that could have sent me home prematurely.

A few years ago, I wrote to Pauline to make sure she knew the difference that she had made to me. The reconnecting conversation was terrific and Pauline is now back in my life.

There's Nothing Splendid About Isolation

When I was doing this with one group, I asked a guy who had helped him as he had grown up. He said that he couldn't think of anyone. He had done it all himself. There is no way he could have achieved what he had done on his own, so he was going around unaware of all the people who had and were helping him to succeed. This meant that people who deserved thanks would go unappreciated. But it also meant that he had no idea how he fitted into a much greater web of relationships. He was going through life believing he was alone–that he was isolated.

Small Drops of SEA

The last exercise was for those who deserved a big thank you. It's also rewarding to do the small ones too. Tom Peters said that the best politician he knew used to close his office door for 30 minutes a day to write thank you notes to the people who had helped him that day. He attributed much of the man's success to this activity. He also said that most thank you notes went to junior people–such as the aide who had arranged the meeting with the congressman and the executive assistant who had squeezed him into the Vice President's diary. These people are most likely to be forgotten.

So, if you appreciate someone or their work, tell them. If you love someone or love what they do, tell him or her and say thank you. If you get great service checking into a hotel or on the last flight home when you're exhausted, write them a short note. Don't do it for the reward, do it to help great people get what they deserve. There's no way of knowing what the little drops of SEA can do. We live in such an appreciation scarce environment today you may be the only person who said thank you to that person this year (seriously).

Connect with Excellence

We have all heard of the saying "*an apple a day keeps the doctor away*," but what do you do to sustain your inspiration levels? How about, "*A masterpiece a day, keeps burn out away*"? Is there a poet you admire? An author? Could you connect with a few lines of their work every day? When was the last time you took a moment to appreciate the mastery in what someone did? It could be a work of art but it could also be the barista making your daily coffee with extraordinary skill. It could be a colleague who has a particularly high level of skill in one part of their work. If you think that, share it with them. The odds are that they will have had to find their own motivation to develop that skill which will not have been recognised by many. And connecting with mastery for its own sake can inspire you to work to improve your mastery, a vital part of your continued success.

Laugh Often

Laughing is one of the best things you can do to regain the perspective we often lose in stressful situations. It's a great way to see what you are OK about as you have to see the bigger picture to find something funny.

Laughing with others also creates group coherence as everyone moves immediately right on the quadrants and they all breathe together (laugh...then breathe). In his book, *My Spiritual Journey*, the Dalai Lama described himself as "*a professional laugher*"[92] He says "*I laugh often, and my laughter is contagious.*" I would say that anyone who laughs authentically infects others.

I had a Buddhist teacher who couldn't stop herself laughing at times. She found this most difficult just after returning from a retreat. She would have to pause the lesson as she was laughing so much.

I sometimes look at what my children are worrying about and it makes me smile and laugh—that someone as perfect could be worried about something so small. I think that may have been what the Buddhist teacher was laughing about—that we are missing the bigger picture so much, it's funny. We are worrying about things that are simply irrelevant—like a giant worrying about an ant. We spend our time trying to control the weather when all we have to do is make better clothing choices.

I have been fortunate in the last few years to spend time with people who have faced extreme hardship. Most laugh more than my other friends who, on the surface, appear to have more to laugh and be cheerful about. Maybe if you are unsure that you will have the chance to look back and laugh, you are more willing to laugh in the moment you do have. I guess it really is a state of mind. I once came across a comment from a comedian who said "*You know how they say, 'One day, we'll look back on this and laugh?' Well, why wait?*" Good advice.

What Can You Find to Laugh About?

If you can't find reasons to laugh at yourself then you really aren't working at it. However, if you still can't, then go on YouTube and watch a video for a minute or read some jokes and spread them about the office (you can subscribe to joke apps). Laugh daily.

We do our organisations a disservice by discouraging laughter and supporting the idea that everything has to be serious to be professional. One of the deepest truths from the Gesundheit Institute (the organisation set up by physician, Patch Adams) was the way you can be professional and still laugh. Take your work extremely seriously but hold yourself lightly.

Perform RAKs Everyday

Another way to stimulate positive emotions and to help others is to perform RAKs (Random Acts of Kindness) every day. These can be small ones, such as leaving a small gift on the desk of a co-worker to making a significant donation to a charity.

There are different levels of giving. One of the clearest descriptions comes from the Jewish faith and the Eight Degrees of Tzedakah as articulated by the 12th century teacher Maimonides. "Tzedakah" is a Hebrew word that refers to what we would call "charity" in English. However, the root of this word means righteousness, justice, or fairness. Giving is not a generous act so much as it is willingly performed duty or act of justice and fairness.

The highest form of giving, according to Maimonides, was to give in such a way that the recipient became self-supporting and no longer needed to rely on others to live. So a loan or grant to pay for someone's education or to help someone by forming a business partnership would be examples of this. This then moves down to anonymous giving (and receiving) and finally to the

eighth and lowest level where the giver offers reluctantly
and usually out of pity.

Act as if You Received Your Call-up Papers

USMC (Ret) Colonel Mike Wyly is Executive
Director of one of the best ballet companies in America,
the Bossov Ballet. They are based in Pittsfield, Maine–
about the least likely place for a world class ballet
company you can imagine. Surprisingly, Mike's love of
ballet came through the Vietnam War.

As he prepared for his second tour in Vietnam, Mike
decided to spend all his salary on every cultural activity
he could find, whether he had a particular interest or
not. He reasoned it may be his last chance, so he tried
the best the Washington, D.C. had to offer. His
experience of ballet triggered a life–long love that
endures today. This love generated his second career
after leaving the USMC as administrator of the Bossov.[93]

My friend Nigel came to a similar level of openness
through a different route. Some years ago he was
diagnosed with cancer. He was in his early forties so this
was a real shock. The prognosis was poor so he and his
wife decided to have one last Christmas before telling
the children. They made it the best they had ever had.
This wasn't so much in presents as in the quality of the
contact and connection they made with friends and
family. At work, Nigel stopped doing things he didn't
find nourishing and focused even more on making a
lasting contribution to everything he did.

Amazingly, his cancer responded to treatment, and he
made a full recovery. But instead of returning to the way
he used to work, he continued to act as if his days were
numbered. He tells me he is much better for it. And
when you think about it, he's right for all of us.

Are you making the best use of your time? If you
were to review your last week and imagined your

interactions were the last you were ever going to have with the people you were with, how differently would you have behaved? If this week were your last, how would you want to act? If the work you were doing was the last you would ever do, would you be happy about that?

One thing I have gained by losing so much financial wealth is the stripping away of priorities I used to think were crucial. I always thought I was fairly purpose driven but now I only want to do work that contributes in some way. I could find a way to motivate myself to work with groups or organisations that were going through the motions. I can't (or won't) anymore. If it doesn't matter, then why bother? Instead of taking the money for work that you aren't motivated to do, why not work to reduce your financial needs, so you can afford to do work that's meaningful and only you can do?

Tim Ferris in his book, *The Four Hour Week*, asks his readers to imagine they were ill and could only work two hours a day. *"What would you do in those two hours?"* Then he asks, *"What you would do if you had only two hours a week?"* Tim's questions and the idea of acting as if you have received your call up papers are all designed to shake you out of the illusion that your resources are infinite. You need to spend them extremely wisely.[94]

Acceptance and Your Own Tribe

My colleague in the USA, Lt Colonel Mike Grice, interviewed some managers for a leadership program. One was a former Marine. When we asked him what we could help the leadership team do more effectively, he said *"Help people feel accepted."* He said:

"Before I went through USMC Officer Training, I wondered if I really belonged. Having completed that

training, I knew I was a Marine and that I would always be a Marine. I had been fully accepted.

"In this organisation, I have done things that were equally hard but I don't feel accepted. I feel as if I am only ever one mistake away from being kicked out. So I have to protect myself instead of going all out."

This links perfectly to the Losada research and Stephen Porges work on safe social environments. Too few corporate environments feel safe enough for someone to take the risks necessary to pursue excellence. So as well as looking to generate and feel more acceptance at work, it may be helpful for you to strengthen your own network inside and outside your company to build your own sense of acceptance.

Seth Godin, the marketing expert, talks about the importance of Tribes[95]–finding and connecting with like-minded people. Finding your own tribe is something that can create a great deal of reassurance and confidence to stretch further. Look out for people like you and find a way of connecting more frequently.

Self-Acceptance

It may be that your company is low on acceptance and, like the Marine, you may feel that you are not accepted. This won't be anything you can change in a short space of time so I would encourage you to work on your own self-acceptance. Most people I work with (especially high-achievers) have a belief that they have never been enough.

Being an insecure over-achiever makes you ill even if the compulsion to deliver keeps you warm most of the time. That's a fire that will burn down your house and everything you value. Work to become a secure over-achiever. Secure over-achievers are happier, make better bosses, and have more long-term success in part because they have taken the time to define success for themselves.

EE Cummings once said to *"to be nobody—but—yourself...is to fight the hardest battle...any human can fight"* as you are being tested all the time to be what you are not.[96] If you find any active acceptance too hard, work to accept the choices you made, and that you probably did the best you could with what you had. Then, if appropriate, get to work making things right.

Feedback as a Way to Show SEA

Another great way to show SEA for others is to offer better quality and more frequent feedback. Think about what you are seeing people do that is improving things and tell them specifically why and how what they did helped and that you want to see more of it.

"Great job. You're amazing" is not particularly helpful feedback. How about:

> *"Sarah, I was impressed with your handling of the tough questions about our proposal. You appeared totally calm when you shared the right data, and you offered to follow up if they had more questions. To me, this showed just how much preparation you had done. Please keep it up and let me know how I can help you if they have more questions."*

Given the theme of this chapter and the importance I have placed on cultivating positive emotions, it will be no surprise for me to encourage you to give far more positive feedback than negative. However, even though we are supposed to enjoy positive feedback, people can resist receiving appreciation or praise. A quick way around that is to make the data-based statement and then ask a question without giving the person a chance to respond with *"It was nothing."*

In the case of Sarah above, you could follow up with, "*Were you really that calm?*" or "*What told you to be ready for those questions?*" The compliment will sink in as she hasn't had chance to reject it and you get her focused on what she did to generate such a strong performance. You can do this as you walk around the office. Just be sincere and authentic.

Who Do You Rely on?

When you look at the people you work with and the people you need to do what you do, how much SEA do they get from you? When was the last time you raised their SEA levels? Some executives tell me that they don't express appreciation to their people as they worry the person may get too high an opinion of themselves. Imagine that, having a team who appreciated their own worth!

The imaginary danger of having confident colleagues aside, showing SEA for someone tends to strengthen that relationship rather than weaken it. As I said at the start of this book, feeling that you are winning or making progress doing work you find meaningful is the biggest motivator and the biggest antidote to negative stress. Telling someone "*Your work matters to me because...*" tops up someone's reserves.

To increase the impact of this further, if you are senior manager, get another senior manager to thank your people personally for their help on a project or sorting out a problem that affected both departments. The value is massive and it costs nothing.

Being Positive in Negative Environments

Behaving more in line with the research into the best teams (positive, supportive, inquiring, and externally focused), can lead colleagues in negative environments to think you are less intelligent. This would be counterproductive to your career development—at least in the short term.

Consider the *"Brilliant, but cruel"* findings from some fascinating research by Teresa Amabile, the Harvard professor who co-developed the Progress Principle. Amabile conducted a study of critics who were either negative (and often cruel) in their assessment of someone's work and other critics who were more positive. Readers of the critiques consistently rated the negative critics as smarter than those adopting a more positive tone (even if there was no objective evidence to support it).

This led her to the *"brilliant, but cruel"* moniker. She concluded, *"Only pessimism sounds profound. Optimism sounds superficial."*[97] *"If you really understood, how could you be positive?"* seems to be the mind-set.

When raising SEA levels, start with:

1. Yourself (especially how you support and encourage yourself)
2. Family and friends
3. Trusted friends at work
4. Trusted colleagues who seem more receptive to this approach
5. Colleagues you respect (privately at first)
6. Review your results before deciding to run meetings on more positively focused grounds

By doing this, you can create your own micro environment that is SEA. As this develops you will gradually become more influential through the organization without being exposed to unnecessary risk.

The Speed of Trust

Relationships are key to any efforts to gain long term success in stressful situations. A strong network of colleagues at work and friends outside help you to defuse any peaks in stress. This is challenging as we seem to be losing the ability to make and keep friends. I have a number of male clients who actually have no friends. One told me I was the only person he could speak to about how things were going other than his wife. I replied that he was paying me to do it and that, as we all know, if you have to pay, it isn't love!

Loneliness has been shown to cause illness. We are drawn to be part of communities. It's how we have evolved to deal with challenging environments. Communities have always been nature's insurance policy against bad events. If we are not in a community, then we have to provide our own sense of security and few of us have the resources for that. I wonder if the isolation most people feel from a genuine community is one of the biggest causes of the stress people feel. If you were able to strengthen your key relationships not only would you have more support when you found yourself in trouble, you'd have less trouble by and large.

Rebecca Merrell and Stephen Covey (the son of the world famous author with the same name) argue that relationships are essential for companies to move quickly enough to capture the fleeting opportunities in our global economy.[98]

Trust allows everyone to move faster which is helpful in dynamic situations. Be aware of the trust you have in key workplace relationships. One key to trust is the alignment of interests over an agreed time frame. The better the relationship, the greater the willingness for someone to forgo short-term gain as they help you. That's the essence of friendships—how long is someone willing to wait to be repaid for their generosity to you? The deepest friendships have shared pots that both parties are committed to keeping full. In such relationships, repayment is increasingly irrelevant as it feels as if your act of SEA in repaying them for being such a great friend.

Become a Student of Friendship and Community

Who are the best friends you have ever had? What made that relationship so special? When you look at your behaviour with them and with most people around you, what differences do you see? What for you was the difference that made the difference?

Talk to some of your best friends about this—ask them what makes a great relationship. Ask how you could be a better friend or, better still, think about it and then do it, and see what a difference it makes.

How to Give and Be Relaxed About Receiving

I used to give to just about anyone who wanted help. I don't anymore. When I got into trouble, I found to my shock that many of the people I thought were friends were merely acquaintances and they just melted away. This was "disconcerting."

Now I care much more about reciprocity than I did. To give without thinking about the return goes against our evolutionary instincts. Reciprocity is the foundation of community, as Bob Cialdini points out in *Influence*.[99] Living in groups of people who support each other and pool resources to achieve larger outcomes creates safe physical and social environments. Now, I try to give only to people who are as committed to giving to me as I am to them.

To avoid having to keep score (which is no way to have a friendship) I am just be more careful about the people I am friends with. This allows me to give them anything they need as I know they will do the same for me. At the start of a relationship, give generously and then reciprocate.

Know Where You Are

You need to look at your relationships and see how much adversity you think they will be able to handle. You can take as active or passive an approach to this as you like. The problem I had wasn't that I had acquaintances. The problem was that I had deluded myself that our relationship was more than that, and I needed friends and not acquaintances when I got into trouble. So look at the relationships around you and decide what they could handle (both ways). Who would you help if they were in trouble? How far would you go? If you can, find ways to test your assumptions. Start by having a conversation with them. Ask how *you* could be a better friend to *them*.

4am Friends

Marlene Dietrich, the Hollywood actress, made an excellent point when she said,

> *"It's the friends you can call up at 4am that matter."*

If you were in trouble, who could you call in the middle of the night and know that help would be offered? I have three, maybe four friends in this category. I feel immensely fortunate to have so many. They are all 20-year plus friendships too. Friendship seems to be a slow growing tree.

One of my 4am friends actually lives in the US, five hours behind London, so she would only be an 11pm friend if I ever needed her! And I would be her 9am friend! One of the benefits of global relationships—if you have friends around the world, no one has to be woken up when you need help!

So how many 4am friends do you have? How many potential 4am friends are you creating? How many 20-year friendships do you have? They are the people who will still be there if everyone else left. They really are very precious. Be sure to treat them with the love and respect they deserve instead of taking them for granted. These form your strongest links in your network. Other links are still crucial so let's look at those now.

Facebook Is Great – Just Remember Its Purpose

My friend Neil got me onto Facebook. He sent my email address to some of my old friends and got them to email me in the same week inviting me to join. He then called to close the deal and told me I couldn't refuse a friendship request. *"Say "Yes" to everyone!"* was his advice. I have mostly stuck with that. If I can't remember someone at all, then I will at least send a note asking how we know each other.

So get onto Facebook and reconnect with your old friends. Remember that FB has to be supplemented with face-to-face meetings. Once you have been on it for a few months and have most of the old crew back together (at least virtually), get on Skype with a few and then meet some of them in person. With at least one old friend, renew your old memories and find the funniest pictures you can of them and you. The success measure is to laugh so much you fall off your chair. My life feels better having people in my life who have known me almost as long as I have. Knowing your own history helps you to recognise your strengths and weaknesses as most of us have had them all our lives.

Helping Your Friends in Tough Times

When bad news hits, the silence afterwards can be utterly shocking. People don't know what to say so they say nothing. This hurts as it makes you feel even more alone. When your friends are in trouble, my advice would be to tell them you don't know what to say but that you are thinking of them. Be the one to call to say how sorry you are, that you are thinking of them, and that you will go round soon. Then visit–immediately if you can.

I once met with a partner in one of the largest consultancies in the world. I was running a seminar on relationships, and he gave the keynote address. The one piece of advice that still stands out today was that he told the young leaders to call someone if they had been fired. If you could, help him or her get a new job.

In some situations there is nothing you can do or say to make things better. Acceptance has to come first and that can take a long time. If you are not sure if it's the right time to offer reassurance of a future, then don't say it. It sounds like such platitudinous rubbish at the wrong time. Would you know how to lift up a friend who had faced the toughest loss of his life? Would you know what to say? Sometimes there is nothing to say when the loss is so great. So sit with him or her, and be ready to help more actively when they are ready.

John Boyd, showed himself to be a friend in tough times. He was willing to fight for the people he cared about. Mike Wyly was rewarded for his tireless service and efforts to improve the USMC by being retired early (fired). He was a full Colonel but he left Quantico with his wife and children and drove to Maine with no retirement ceremony. He told me it was a shocking time for him, but John Boyd was there. They spoke every day and Boyd even used a Congressional Hearing to express his dismay at the way Mike Wyly had been treated. This wasn't in Boyd's short-term interests, but he did it because the friendship meant that much to him. What friendships would you risk your professional career for?

Summary

- Positive psychology is the field of psychology that finds ways to promote flourishing.
- Research by Fredrickson and Losada show that having three positive emotional experiences for every negative one enables flourishing.
- Positivity has a number of benefits. It broadens our minds and perceptions and allows us to be more creative. And it builds resources that make us more able to deal with tough situations.
- Top teams have higher SEA levels than average teams-they are more supportive, encouraging and appreciative. This creates a safe environment for team members to stretch to succeed.
- The research also highlights the importance of an appropriately negative perspective to help people remain grounded and how insincere positivity can be worse than authentic negativity.
- An easy way to raise SEA levels is to say thank you to people you care about and who have helped you.
- Connecting with excellence and finding reasons to laugh are two other ways to do this.
- It is important to be careful when you increase SEA levels in historically negative environments. Build a micro–climate before you try to change the weather.
- Becoming a student of friendship and community can help us to be more supportive and attract more support.

- In becoming a better friend, it's important to find people who care for you as you do for them.
- The most precious friends are "*4am friends*"—the friends you could call on day or night to ask for help and know that it will be there.
- You can show your greatest strengths by being a friend in tough times—a 4am friend to others.

12.
Conclusion/Beginning

I had planned to do a summary chapter for this book. As I got closer to the end, it didn't seem appropriate. My purpose was to help you have a better 90 days by improving your ability to adapt to, and then anticipate turbulence in your chosen environments. This frees up resources for you to get ahead of what is happening and to shape your environment which affects what you and those you care about will face in 3-12 months. So I don't want you to see this as a conclusion of anything but a beginning. What beginning it is, is entirely up to you.

Stay in touch

Be sure to check out www.stressandsuccess.com where I continue the work we have started here and offer more resources and support.

If you have any questions regarding the content in this book or the challenge you are facing feel free to email me at jb@alppartners.com.

When I reflect on my actions as I have recovered from the burn out I experienced, I feel I have made most progress through my role as a parent. The next is being a 4am friend to a handful of friends and helping them to transform the momentum in the situations they were facing. And then it's with the clients who have faced tough times and trusted me enough to either embrace success or to help them recover so fast they avoided the trouble I had.

The common thread running through all of those situations is the desire to be someone who gets better as the situation gets worse. I think that is the most rewarding role anyone can play. I hope I have increased your skill and desire to do the same.

Thank You

Four groups have played a crucial role in helping me take my experiences further. Firstly I'd like to thank my colleagues and clients past and present for being willing to try some crazy ideas that turned out to help them be even more successful.

The second group are some extraordinary people connected to the US Armed Forces. I'd like to thank members of the USMC especially Colonel Mike Wyly (Ret.), leader of the only ballet company run along US Marine Corp lines-The Bossov! And Lt. Colonel Mike Grice (Ret) who is an inspiring leader.

Two people were especially helpful and just happened to be catalysts for the world's largest psychological initiative, Comprehensive Soldier Fitness Program. Colonel Jill Chambers (US Army-Ret) is insightful, witty, and patient. Her pioneering work helping US service members with PTS inspires me to serve others. And Professor Mike Matthews at the US Military Academy, West Point. Mike's openness, hospitality and wisdom in his correspondence and in the subsequent visit to West Point are things I will long remember. Thank you both for your help and your continued inspiration.

Mary Ellen Boyd and the Boyd family were generous in allowing me to use their father's material; Chet Richards is wise, generous and witty in equal measure; and thanks to the Boyd and Beyond Group for their thoughts and the invitation to speak at the 2012 Boyd Conference at USMCB Quantico.

To the design and editing team. Kathy, Karen, Steven, Annie, Stuart and Tom. Many, many thanks! You did the best with what I gave you and I love what you did with it. Thanks also to Daniel, a surprising and most welcome source of help and inspiration at a crucial time. All the mistakes are mine! Thanks also to the friends who gave such thoughtful comments about the early editions.

My final thank you goes to my family. The last five years have been both wonderful and incredibly difficult. Thankfully, we get far more wonderful than difficult these days. I can't express how grateful I am for your support when all we had was difficulty. Some storms are so bad that only the brightest lights on shore offer any chance of return.

To all of you, especially Tom, Jess, Jane and Jean, your lights brought me home.

About the Author

Jonathan Brown began his professional career with Procter & Gamble. He has run his own consultancy since 2003. He now works with some of the world's top firms helping them to adapt to, and then shape, rapidly changing situations (especially when results are needed quickly).

He received a degree in Japanese and Economics from Sheffield University and lives in Surrey, England with his wife, and two children. At weekends, when not driving his busy children around, he can be found cycling in the Surrey Hills.

This is his first book.

He can be reached at jb@alppartners.com.

Notes

[1] Maybe I should copyright that phrase? - Consider this the first book ever written on *Stress Leadership*™!

[2] Selye, H. (1976). *The Stress of Life* (Revised Edition), Montreal: McGraw Hill, p. xvi.

[3] You could also describe this as single and double loop learning as defined by the extraordinarily productive Chris Argyris and Donald Schon. There is more about them available on the SAS website.

[4] Mr Buffett has managed an average return on investment of 20% a year. There's nothing remarkable in that on a year by year basis. The utterly staggering thing is that he has done it for nearly 50 years in a row. He is famous for being the best investor in the world. I think he deserves the title of best manager also. Along with Jim Stockdale, a man worthy of deep study.

[5] Jeffrey Pfeiffer and Bob Sutton write brilliant books on their own and in partnership. Bob Sutton has an excellent blog too. Both are committed to writing what is true instead of what is new or most palatable. Pfeiffer co-wrote a stunning book in 1978 that called into question the idea that an organization actually controlled its own future. *The External Control of Organisations* is one of the most significant management books in my library and, like any truly great work, is mostly ignored today. The laws I quoted here are from their 2006 book, *Hard Facts, Dangerous Half-Truths & Total Nonsense.* Boston: HBR Press. They debunk just about every popular management myth going so avoid if you want to continue believing in the Emperor's invisible suit.

[6] I first came across this phrase in Ronald Wright's 2004 book, *A Short History of Progress.* I use it with essentially the same meaning but for individuals or organisations instead of societies. That is, "solving" a problem today which, due to unforeseen consequences, creates a bigger problem in the future.

[7] Amabile, T. and Kramer, S. (2011). *The Progress Principle.* Boston: HBR Press.

[8] John Boyd, (2006) The Strategic Game of ? and ? © Col John R. Boyd estate.

[9] USMC, (2007). *Warfighting.* New York: Cosimo Publishing, P5-6.

[10] Popper, K. (1999) *All Life is Problem Solving.* (Trans. Patrick Camiller. London: Routledge. P100

[11] Michael Grinder, one of the world's best teachers, introduced me to this.

[12] Argyris, C. and Schon, D. (1996) *Organisational Learning II: Theory, Method, and Practice.* Reading, Mass: Addison Wesley Publishing. P31-32. Peter Drucker also says something similar in many of his books.

[13] Personal conversation with author.

[14] Nietzsche, F. (1968). *Twilight of the Idols.* London: Penguin Classics p33. Nietzsche is still relevant today, especially if you face challenging times. His work has been grossly distorted over the years but it has much merit.

[15] I got this idea from the philosopher Karl Popper who wrote an essay *"All life is problem solving."* So now I am aiming to help you be happier, more fulfilled and philosophically rigorous!

[16] Schon, D.A. (1971). *Beyond the Stable State.* New York: Random House.

[17] Sweeney, P.J. Matthews, M.D. Lester, P.J. (Eds). (2011). *Leadership in Dangerous Situations. Annapolis:* Naval Institute Press. Mike Matthews is one of the smartest people I have ever had the privilege to meet and the summary chapter he has written with Pat Sweeney is one of the best essays on leadership I have ever read.

[18] Porges, S.W. (2011). *The Polyvagal Theory: Neurophysiological Foundations of Emotion, Attachment, Communication, and Self-Regulation.* New York: W.W. Norton & Co.

[19] Sarasvathy, S.D. (2008). *Effectuation.* Cheltenham: Edward Elgar Publishing. Sarasvathy's work is brilliant but this work is aimed at an academic audience and is a tough read in places. I will be writing more about this method in the second book. For now though, consider work from the faculty at Babson College in Boston who use her work as part of the top entrepreneurial education in the USA. Babson's President, Len Schlesinger, has co-written an excellent primer on this topic called *Just Start* (2012).

[20] http://www.wired.com/magazine/2011/11/ff_bezos/4/

[21] This quote is attributed to the rocket scientist Wernher von Braun. I have been unable to find the actual reference.

[22] Adapted from Ness, J. Jablonski-Kaye, D. Obigt, I and Lam, D. *Understanding and Managing Stress,* in Sweeney, P.J. Matthews, M.D. Lester, P.J. (Eds). (2011). P52

[23] Yerkes R.M. and Dodson J.D. (1908). *"The relation of strength of stimulus to rapidity of habit-formation."* Journal of Comparative Neurology and Psychology 18: 459–482

[24] Conversation with author, Maine, USA, 2011. Colonel Mike Wyly was at the centre of the USMC transformation and recovery

from the Vietnam War in the 1980s. He was one of the authors of the USMC military doctrine, *Warfighting* and was a long-time friend and colleague of John Boyd. His help and generosity turned a moderate interest in military strategy into an intense one.

[25] Swank, R.L. and Marchand, W.E. (1946). "*Combat Neurosis: Development of Combat Exhaustion.*" American Medical Association: Archives of Neurology and Psychiatry.

[26] Grossman, D.A. (Lt Col) (2009). *On Killing: The Psychological Cost of Learning to Kill in War and Society* (Revised). New York: Back Bay Books. p44. Dave Grossman's rigourous and thoughtful approach to this difficult topic makes for terrific if deeply disturbing reading. A true intellectual committed to making a difference.

[27] Attributed to Harold Macmillan, UK Prime Minister, in response to being asked what he feared most as Prime Minister.

[28] Selye, H. (1976). P370.

[29] Sullenberger, S. with Zaslow, J. *Highest Duty: My Search for What Matters Most.* New York: William Morrow. P237

[30] Ursin, H. Baade, E. and Levine, T. 1978. *Psychobiology of Stress: A Study of Coping Men,* Ed, New York: Academic Press. I had seen frequent references to this study but only tracked it down when I was writing this book. I regret taking so long to read it. It is one of the finest I have ever encountered. Holger Ursin was gracious in answering my questions and continues to lead his field today.

[31] It also involves such things as increased testosterone, catecholamine, growth hormone, free fatty acids, and blood glucose.

[32] Perkins, C.C. Jr. (1968). *An analysis of the concept of reinforcement.* Psychological Review, 75, PP155-172.

[33] Seligman, M.E.P. (1968) *Chronic fear produced by unpredictable electric shock.* Journal of Comparative and Physiological Psychology, 66, PP402-411.

[34] Ursin, H. Baade, E. and Levine, T. (1978). P211.

[35] Jean Paul Satre said some interesting things on this topic if you want to read more.

[36] Semler, R. (2003). *The Seven Day Weekend.* London: Century.P1

[37] DeMarco, T. (2001) *Slack: Getting Past Burnout, Busywork, and the Myth of Total Efficiency.* New York: Broadway Books.

[38] Epictetus. (1995), *The Discourses.* London: Everyman. P.179. I started reading Epictetus as Jim Stockdale credited his philosophy with giving him the philosophical strength to survive his time in captivity. I think I now prefer this to Marcus Aurelius' Meditations but either is a great way to start the day.

[39] Conversation with author, August 2011, Maine, USA.

[40] Ackoff, R.L. (1981) *Creating the Corporate Future: Plan or be Planned For.* New York: John Wiley & Sons. Peter Drucker also emphasised that you didn't need to predict the future but simply to understand the consequences of our present actions in many of his books.

[41] I will be covering this in much more detail in Chapter 9.

[42] Porras, J., Emery, S., and Thompson, M., (2007) *Success Built to Last: Creating a Life That Matters.* London: Plume Books. This is one of the best books I have ever read on success. It has some fantastic insights from the broadest spectrum of successful people that I have ever seen in a book of this nature. It's practical, insightful, and brilliantly written.

[43] Buckingham, M. and Coffman, C. (1999) *First, Break All The Rules: What the World's Greatest Managers Do Differently.* London: Simon & Schuster UK Ltd. Along with Bob Cialdini's *Influence*, FBATR is the book I have recommended most to my clients over the last 10 years. If you are pressed for time, start with the CD. It's brilliant and redefined what "thorough" means for business books.

[44] In fact, a disproportionate number of retired Marines sign their correspondence *"Semper Fi."* They mean that their word is true, as are they.

[45] The Strategic Game of ? and ?, Boyd Estate, 2003

[46] Warren Buffett said this in a speech to MBA students at the University of Florida in 1998. You can watch the speech here. http://www.youtube.com/watch?v=BfPstvyyC1Q. He says this at 5.06 mins. [Pete Kiewit, the man Buffett mentions ran a local construction company that branched out into mining and engineering. It is now a global business.]

[47] Whilst I do not draw directly from his work in this chapter, my understanding of stress has been improved dramatically by the work of Robert Sapolsky.

[48] This phrase was created by Walter Cannon, a Harvard professor who discovered the process in the 1930s and wrote about it in a book called *The Wisdom of the Body.* Some of his ideas have since been found to be incorrect thanks to advances in medical testing and analysis, but his work and contribution to our understanding of stress was immense.

[49] Damasio, A. (2000). *The Feeling of What Happens: Body, Emotion, and the Making of Consciousness.* London: Vintage Books.

[50] I achieved a black belt in judo when I lived in Japan. "Judo" can be translated into English as "The Soft or Gentle Way." The

motto of my judo club was "*Softness can overcome hardness.*" I don't believe there was any irony or double entendre intended.

[51] I was first introduced to a variation of this model about 10 years ago by Dr Alan Watkins, a terrific British physician. Alan was pivotal in validating the science behind Heart Math or cardiac coherence. He called this model Henry's Axis after Dr James Henry, who developed the concepts of the way stress and emotions interact. Since then I have seen other versions of it, none of which were attributed to Dr. Henry. I have read some of Henry's work but have been unable to determine the original source material so I don't know if it came from Henry. However, I have always found Alan to be utterly scrupulous and rigorous in his attribution of credit.

The most impressive evolution of this model comes from the Institute of HeartMath in their 2006 e-book, *The Coherent Heart.* In it they have integrated another decade of research and have far more information regarding the specific emotional states and the effect on someone's physiology and thinking.

[52] The only time you can expect no variability (for any length of time) is just prior to death. If your HRV goes to zero, your life tends to do the same.

[53] If you want to learn more about this there are two great chapters in Servan-Schreiber, D. (2005) *Healing Without Freud or Prozac: Natural Approaches to Curing Stress, Anxiety, and Depression.* London: Chandos. The rest of the book is just as good too. You can also read any E-Books by The Institute of HeartMath or Childre, D. & Martin, H. with Beech, D. (1999) *The HeartMath Solution: Proven Techniques for Developing Emotional Intelligence* or their "Transforming...[Emotions]" Series.

[54] Unpublished research into the efficacy of an HM program. Shared with the author.

[55]Secunda, B. and Allen, M. (2010) *Fit Soul, Fit Body: 9 Keys to a Healthier, Happier You.* Dallas: Benbella Books Inc.

[56] Conversation with author, 2011.

[57] Kolditz, T. 2007. *In Extremis Leadership – Leading as if Your Life Depended on It.* New York: John Wiley & Sons. P223.

[58] Selye, H. (1976).

[59] Pollan, M. (2009). *Food Rules: An Eater's Manual.* London: Penguin Books.

[60] Cleave, T.L. (1974). *The Saccharine Disease: Conditions Caused by the Taking of Refined Carbohydrates, such as Sugars and White Flour.* New Canaan: Keats Publishing Inc.

[61] Kenton, L. (2002). *Age Power*. London: Vermillion.

[62] Conversation with author, 2012.

[63] Churchill, W. (1923). *The World Crisis*, vol. 2 *1915*. London: Thornton Butterworth. p21. I am indebted to Richard Langworth CBE, one of the world's leading authorities on Churchill, for his help in identifying and contextualizing this quotation.

[64] Sun Tzu. (2009). *The Art of War: Denma Translation*. Boston: Shambhala. There are many different translations of The Art of War as it is known in the West. The Denma translation is my favourite. The book has a number of exceptional essays which can deepen your understanding and appreciation of the text. One of the editors, Barry Boyce, also writes on mindfulness.

[65] General Paul Van Riper became famous for demolishing US forces in the world's most expensive military exercise–a $250m simulation in which US forces invaded Iraq. Playing the role of a maverick Middle East leader, he used the principles of maneuver warfare to defeat a numerically superior US Joint Force. This was documented in Malcolm Gladwell's Blink (2005). He also played a key role in rewriting the USMC doctrine, *Warfighting*.

[66] Years after his passing, Boyd remains a controversial figure for a number of reasons. His work takes effort to understand, he was famously abrasive in his dealings with others, and he deliberately left no definitive text. However, it has found its way into some management works such as *Re-imagine* by Tom Peters. The best business book using Boydian principles is Chet Richard's *Certain to Win*, a book Chet wrote with Boyd. Chet is as approachable and kind as he is insightful. If you want to learn more about Boyd and his work, Robert Coram's peerless biography is the place to go: Coram, R. 2002. *Boyd–The Fighter Pilot Who Changed The Art of Warfare*. New York: Little, Brown and Company.

[67] Boyd is usually given all the credit for this. However, he was always clear that this work was collaboration with Tom Christie. Christie's mathematical and political skills allowed them to test the theory at Eglin Air Force Base in Florida.

[68] The Strategic Game of ? and ?, © Boyd Estate. 2006.

[69] This has been attributed to Einstein in many different articles and books. I have been unable to find the source though. To honour the convention, I recognise the probable source as Einstein (and maybe John Dryden).

[70] Ackoff, R. (1981).

[71] Reproduced with kind permission of the Boyd Estate.

[72] Conversation with author at the Boyd Archives in MCB Quantico, October 2012.

[73] Argyris, C. and Schon, D. (1996). P31

[74] Weick, K.E. and Sutcliffe, K.M. (2007) *Managing the Unexpected: Resilient Performance in an Age of Uncertainty (Second Edition).* Hoboken: John Wiley and Sons. p18.

[75] Taleb, N.N. (2008). *The Black Swan: The Impact of the Highly Improbable.* London: Penguin.

[76] Roberto, M.A. (2009) *Know What You Don't Know: How Great Leaders Prevent Problems Before They Happen.* New Jersey: Prentice Hall.

[77] Klein, G. 2003. *The Power of Intuition.* New York: Doubleday. P99-100. Additional material from communication with author.

[78] Hans Selye was the first to highlight this.

[79] Rogers, C. (1961) *On Becoming a Person.* New York: Houghton Mifflin. p25. Rogers is one of the most influential therapists of the 20th Century. His insights also formed a massive part of the modern coaching movement yet largely go unnoticed in part I think because he was so good at helping people discover their own wisdom and because he seemed to have little or no need for others to see how good he was! This quote comes from his essay, "*This is Me,*" is well worth a read. He had one of the strongest commitments to learning that I have ever studied. A brilliant man.

[80] Collins, J. (2001) *Good to Great.* New York: Harper Collins. P88.

[81] Stockdale, J. (1995).*Thoughts of a Philosophical Fighter Pilot.* Stanford: Hoover Institution Press. p11. I would like to thank the Stockdale Family for their kind permission to use this work.

[82] Stockdale is a must-read for students of leadership. He is one of the few writers who has changed my perspective on life. I recommend all of his work. I'd suggest beginning with his essays in *Thoughts of a Philosophical Fighter Pilot,* and move onto *In Love and War* (written with his wife who was an amazing leader herself). *Foundations of Moral Obligation – The Stockdale Course* written by Joseph Gerard Brennan gives more of his philosophical insights – especially the Stoic philosophers. Also, if you really want to understand The Stockdale Perspective, you need to read Epictetus and the other stoic philosophers. If you are facing difficulties, Discourses can be used as a life raft.

[83] Rock, D. 2009. *Your Brain at Work.* New York: Harper Collins.

[84] Ibid, p112

[85] Wellington, C. 2012 *A Life Without Limits.* London: Constable & Robinson Ltd.

[86] Seligman has probably done more than anyone to promote psychological well-being or flourishing. He also played a central role

in developing the US military's Comprehensive Soldier Fitness Program, to which he still gives his time for free. To find out more, read: Seligman, M.E.P, (2011). *Flourish: A New Understanding of Happiness and Well Being – And How To Achieve Them.* London: Nicholas Brearley Publishing.

[87] Fredrickson, B.L. and Losada, M.F. (2005). *Positive Affect and the Complex Dynamic of Human Flourishing,* American Psychologist, October 2005. PP679 – 686.

[88] This was known as the Losada Ratio in some texts. However, he appears to have played down that in favour of the Positivity Ratio as cited in Fredrickson and Losada, 2005.

[89] Fredrickson, B. (2009). *Positivity: Ground-breaking Research to Release Your Inner Optimist and Thrive.* Oxford: One World Publications.

[90] Barbara Ehrenreich makes some excellent arguments in this area in *Brightsided.* Even though I think many of the authors she disputes have simply been misinterpreted, her core argument, that a falsely positive view of life does more damage than good, is an excellent one.

[91] Newton said this in a letter to fellow scientist Robert Hooke in 1676, but is believed to have taken it from earlier sources such as John of Salisbury in Metalogicon, 1159. He was standing on their shoulders when he said it – nicely done.

[92] Dalai Lama with Stril-Rever, S. (2009) *My Spiritual Journey.* New York: Harper Collins. P24.

[93] Check out www.bossovballet.com. The board of directors are an extraordinary bunch and they make me wonder if the whole thing is really a front for the CIA...but I think they are simply friends of Colonel Wyly's!

[94] Ferris, T. (2009). *The 4-Hour Work Week: Escape 9-5, Live Anywhere, and Join the New Rich.* New York: Crown Publishing. P80. Tim Ferris' work is excellent. This one is great for practical advice on freeing up your resources.

[95] Godin, S. (2008). *Tribes.* New York: Piatkus.

[96] Cummings, E.E. *A Poet's Advice to Students.* in E. E. Cummings: a Miscellany " Firmage, G.J. (ed.) (1958). New York: Harcourt Brace Javanovich Inc.

[97] Amabile, T. (1983) *"Brilliant but Cruel: Perception of Negative Evaluators,"* Journal of Experimental Social Psychology, 19, P146-156.

[98] Covey, M.R. and Merrell, R. (2006) *The Speed of Trust: The One Thing That Changes Everything.* London: Simon & Schuster.

[99] Cialdini, R.B. (2009) *Influence: Science and Practice. (Fifth Edition)*. Boston: Pearson Education Inc. This is one of the best books I have read in the last 15 years. It can be a little too thorough at times though. However, he seems to have taken some advice from Dan Pink and created a comic book version. Incredibly, you get all the principles without all the theoretical support so read the comic first and go back to the original if you want more.

Lightning Source UK Ltd.
Milton Keynes UK
UKOW050300230313

208075UK00006B/109/P